TOLERATION

TOLERATION

NICK FOTION and GERARD ELFSTROM

The University of Alabama Press ◆ Tuscaloosa & London

Copyright © 1992

The University of Alabama Press

Tuscaloosa, Alabama 35487–0380

All rights reserved

Manufactured in the United States of America

∞

designed by zig zeigler

The paper on which this book is printed

meets the minimum requirements of

American National Standard

for Information Science-Permanence of Paper

for Printed Library Materials,

ANSI Z39.48–1984

Library of Congress Cataloging-in-Publication Data

Fotion, N.

Toleration / Nick Fotion and Gerard Elfstrom.

p.   cm.

Includes bibliographical references and index.

ISBN 0–8173–0581–5 (alk. paper)

1. Toleration.   I. Elfstom, G. (Gerard) II. Title.

BJ1431.F68 1992

179'.9—dc20   91–46331

British Library Cataloguing-in-Publication Data available

0-8173-1193-9 (pbk: alk. paper)

Contents

Preface

All of us have learned well how to tolerate. We tolerate the behavior of our siblings, children, spouse, employer, employees, friends, and strangers. What we tolerate from one or more of these individuals may include heavy drinking, bad breath, sexual advances, nagging, lack of attention, absence of love and affection, lying, infidelity, stupidity, rudeness, a boring personality, incessant chatter, gluttony, indecision, and dominating behavior. But our skills in tolerating are not limited to our relations with individuals. In our relationships with groups we are all experts at tolerating noise, commercials, crime, pollution, high prices, automation, religious practices, racism, sexism, ethnic self-praise, political activities, and God knows what else.

To make matters worse, many people are not satisfied with our present level of toleration. We are urged by some to be more tolerant than we are with respect to the behavior of this individual or with the policies or behavior of that group. Or they even urge us to do more than tolerate—as it were, to transcend it. Others, to confuse things, urge us to be less tolerant or even intolerant in one way or another.

With all the tolerating we do, and with talk about doing more or less of it, the wonder is that philosophers have had so little to say about the concept. In the early portion of the twentieth century, philosophers seemed to be partial toward analyzing 'good', 'duty', and 'obligation', as if understanding one or more of these concepts was the key to understanding ethics and values generally. More recently, in days when philosophers are more concerned with normative issues, analyses of 'justice' and 'right(s)' are in vogue. But surely by now we know enough about how families of concepts work to know that, even if key concepts exist within a family, they cannot be understood without understanding the other family members as well. How important the concept of toleration is, within whatever family or families it belongs, remains to be seen. However, we take it as given that this concept is a sufficiently important member of the family of ethical and political concepts to deserve more attention than it is receiving from philosophers. One main purpose of this study, then, is to direct attention to a generally overlooked and misunderstood concept. Another is to show that this concept is far more complex and interesting than is commonly supposed.

In attending to the concept of toleration, we do not limit ourselves to analyzing 'toleration' and its many cognates. Other expressions or concepts of a more common sort also need attention. We frequently say of a man whom we tolerate that we can stand him, and when we are intolerant we say we cannot stand him. In addition we commonly assert that we can or cannot put up with, or can or cannot abide, someone. Furthermore, toleration is closely related to the concept of freedom, inasmuch as when we tolerate we refrain from depriving others of their freedom. It is also, as we shall see, a near kin of the concept of acceptance. We are assuming that the concept of toleration encompasses or is closely related to all these concepts and others as well. The fact that some of these other expressions can be used in place of 'toleration' may help to explain why it has been given so little attention by philosophers. Another possible reason for its relative invisibility is that tolerating is apparently something we do, paradoxically enough, passively. Whatever it is to tolerate, in large part it implies letting others act (or not act) in the sense of doing little or nothing to interfere with them. So it may be that tolerating in its very quiet way does not get noticed because philosophers tend to concentrate their analyses upon more outspoken concepts.

But it is not just philosophers who ignore the concept of toleration. As we will see (in chap. 7), there are reasons why ordinary people also pass it over in favor of concepts that allow them to think in terms of extremes of right or wrong. There are also reasons why they tolerate much more than they realize. In our study, therefore, we will examine this concept that gets overlooked so readily both by philosophers and by ordinary people.

We do so by analyzing the concept of toleration and its family members in Part I (chaps. 1–5). These discussions are sometimes technical. However, we encourage the reader to work through them, as we believe the analyses of this portion are crucial for fully comprehending the discussions of the second portion of our work. In Part II we examine a variety of topics, beginning with a brief look at the history of the issues that surround the concept (in chap. 6). Next (in chaps. 7 and 8) we look at the contemporary scene, trying to understand why it is that the concept is so important and yet gets overlooked and misunderstood and why certain political thinkers see so little merit to tolerating others (chap. 9). Finally, we will offer an overview (chap. 10) to see where we have gone.

One place we will not have gone is down the path, favored by many contemporary philosophers, of making normative recommendations. Though the reader will quickly discover we are often in sympathy with tolerant responses to certain contemporary issues, our main concern is not that of prescribing how we ought to behave or what we ought to think. Rather, we are content to encourage philosophers and the general public to look more carefully at the concept of toleration (and its family members) so that they will be less likely to overlook and/or misunderstand it when they are called upon to deal with practical problems of both the moral and the nonmoral variety.

Part 1

ANALYSIS

Tolerating, Tolerance, and Intolerance

1

Attitudes and Dispositions

We open the discussion of toleration by characterizing, in a preliminary way, the concepts of tolerating, tolerance, and intolerance. A large portion of the confusion that infects our understanding of toleration results from our failure to distinguish clearly these concepts.[1] Indeed, the principal thesis of this chapter is that they are distinct from one another. We shall argue that an individual who *tolerates* even a good many things is not necessarily a *tolerant* person and that a tolerant person can, at least on some occasions, fail to practice toleration.

These concepts will be distinguished from one another by the differing relationships that they have to our attitudes, dispositions, and actions. For our present purposes, an attitude may be understood simply and crudely as an individual's relatively stable, mental response, either positive or negative, to something. It is not always easy to understand what attitudes per se are. Sometimes they seem to be the simple, uncomplicated responses that we make to something. However, attitudes are not just responses or feelings but appear necessarily to contain a judgmental aspect, although this aspect need not be either rational, deliberative, or even conscious. The fact that Doakes dislikes the taste of broccoli or that he is repelled by the thought of medical surgery does not necessarily indicate what his attitudes are. Doakes may be visibly repulsed by the taste of broccoli, but if he thinks eating it is necessary for his good health, we would not say that he has a negative attitude toward it. Bare physiological responses are not attitudes. It seems that in order to have an

3

attitude, Doakes must have made a judgment that he is satisfied with his immediate responses.

A disposition may be understood simply as a tendency to perform or refrain from performing a particular action. Attitudes and dispositions are not always closely linked either psychologically or physiologically. A negative attitude toward something need not result in a disposition to injure or destroy it. A positive attitude toward something need not result in a disposition to acquire, assist, or safeguard it. It is just this possibility of disjunction between attitude, disposition, and, ultimately, action that helps make tolerating and tolerance interesting—and confusing—concepts.[2]

Tolerating

Tolerating is a transitive concept in that it requires the existence of something tolerated. We cannot tolerate in a vague way, that is, without being able to describe what it is that we tolerate. This is not to say that we must have full comprehension or a thorough knowledge of what we tolerate, but only that we must know something exists that we must endure. The types of things we may tolerate are quite diverse. They include actions, beliefs, attitudes, persons, animals, physical objects, institutions, and conditions. Furthermore, the reasons or motives we have for tolerating these things are varied. We may tolerate from fear, laziness, moral conviction, and/or desire for pragmatic advantage.

In order to be able to say that we tolerate something, it must affect us negatively in some manner. We must have a certain negative attitude toward it, one of dislike or disapproval, or it must cause us discomfort or inconvenience in some way that we may assume will cause us to have a negative attitude toward it. It only makes sense to say that Grundy tolerates Republicans if he dislikes or disapproves of them. If

4

he is fond of Republicans, respects their views and programs, we would not say that he tolerates them. Similarly, it would not make much sense to observe that Grundy tolerates the dentist's drilling on his teeth if the drilling causes him no pain or discomfort or if Grundy is a masochist and enjoys the rigors of his trips to the dentist's chair.

It is not necessary that one must be directly affected by, or in close physical proximity to, what is tolerated. Jenks, ensconced on his farm in Nebraska, may be deeply upset by the thought of nude, communal bathing in California, even though he has never been near that state and has no intention of going there. Nevertheless, Jenks can be said to tolerate such activity if he has consciously made the decision to refrain from expressing his outrage whether by writing indignant letters to newspapers, complaining to passersby, buying billboard space to express his views, or taking other action to combat that which displeases him.

Notice that in this example we need not even say that Jenks is in a position to disrupt that which upsets him. It has been suggested, as a necessary condition of toleration, that we must be able to do something to affect that which we tolerate.[3] This view rests on a confusion. It makes perfectly good sense to say of Lowder, whose AIDS has progressed beyond hope of cure, that he is tolerating his condition quite well, or of Bamberg, confined in an impregnable fortress, that he is tolerating his incarceration. In each of these situations the individual in question tolerates his hopeless condition because we know quite well what it would be like for him not to tolerate it: namely, to rage hopelessly against his fate.

It is usually the case that those who tolerate passively endure that which is unsettling them. The idea of passive endurance is difficult to describe precisely. However, its basic features are that people have negative attitudes regarding certain things but do not vigorously express these attitudes or take action against the objects of their feelings.

5

In these kinds of cases, it is important to understand what passive endurance does not imply as well as what it does. It does not imply acceptance of what is tolerated, in the sense of acknowledging its value or right to exist. Neither does it imply that we have any special moral conviction that demands our quiescence. The negative character of our definition is important here. Passive endurance means simply not expressing disfavor or taking action against what one tolerates. The presence or absence of toleration is closely conceptually linked not with the presence or absence of any particular actions but mainly with a particular conjunction of attitudes and inaction. However, we shall see in later chapters that this initial characterization is overly simple and that there are several modes of enduring, some more and some less passive.

The complexities of describing tolerating nicely illustrate the complexities of the thought and action of human beings. These complexities have been too frequently overlooked in contemporary moral theory, where the model of the agent is that of one who decides, on the basis of reason and evidence, what is to be done and goes out and does it. Sometimes authors will worry about the effects of weakness of will or the problems of responding to skeptics or the immoral, but they find very little complexity in moral activity beyond these issues. However, our analysis has already disclosed a number of distinct levels or areas of mental activity that work on one another in intricate ways. One level is our immediate physiological or emotional response. We are hurt, disgusted, repulsed, nauseated, or whatever. These responses are only transformed into attitudes when, on a different level, we decide either to endorse or override our elemental reflexes.

Not all elemental responses become the basis of attitudes. Lower creatures may lack the mental ability for such endorsement, while humans often pass over their immediate twinges and feelings without judging them. A person idly waiting for a bus, for example, may hazily experience a string of agreeable and noxious sensations without pausing to decide what to think about them.

Often the judgment that transforms a response into an attitude will be nearly as reflexive and unthinking as the original experience. We commonly affirm or deny our feelings with the automatic gesture of a bored teller endorsing a check. Sometimes, of course, attitudes result from careful deliberation, but they need not, and this is part of the reason they are so plastic.

The relationship between attitude and action yields another level of complexity. A person with a negative attitude about one thing or another, even a strongly negative one, need not be disposed to translate that attitude into action. It is all too easy to walk across a sagging porch day in and day out, suffering anxiety and irritation each time, without ever deciding to do anything about it. On a slightly more elevated level, people may take strong and irritated exception to political corruption or incompetence without ever feeling the inclination to instigate change.

Sometimes, of course, people come to have negative attitudes and are disposed to act upon them but do not. This is the classical instance of tolerating. But what prevents action in these cases? The explanation is found in yet another level of mental life, for humans possess the ability to hold their attitudes and dispositions in check and do so for identifiable reasons. We will examine these in detail in chapter 3. For now, it is worth noting that these reasons can be quite diverse, so diverse that it may be misleading to place them on one level, as though they are all of the same sort. For example, our attitudes and dispositions are sometimes held in check by fear or horror, the most primitive of responses. On other occasions they may be overcome by lofty moral principles, as concern for the freedom or autonomy of others. What is clear is that we have an extra layer of interaction and that it forms the basis of tolerating.

Our understanding of toleration implies that people may fail to tolerate in either of two ways. First, they cannot be said to tolerate something if they either actively attempt to hinder, disrupt, or destroy it or if they vigorously express attitudes of contempt, disapproval, or reprobation. Grundy does not tolerate Republicans if he does what he can to disrupt their activities and/or expresses his contempt for them at every opportunity. Furthermore, he does not tolerate something if he either actively assists or furthers its development or if he expresses attitudes of praise or approbation for it. If Grundy spontaneously wrests the drill from his dentist's hands and grinds his own teeth, he can no longer be said to tolerate the drilling, even though his self-dentistry may substantially increase his pain and discomfort. Or, if Grundy extols the virtues and the toughening effect of occasionally suffering a little drilling, he is no longer tolerating it.

This much having been said, it must be acknowledged that in concrete situations it may often be difficult to determine exactly when passive endurance shades off into active hindrance or positive abetting. If Kilgore, for example, grumbles about his teenage son's driving habits, but nonetheless continues to buy him gasoline and hands over the car every Saturday night, does he tolerate such behavior or not? Or if he hands over the car but takes his son out to teach him proper driving habits and elicits vows of careful driving before he turns Junior loose, does he still tolerate it?

This discussion, brief though it is, positions us to locate some of the unusual features that tolerating possesses when considered as a moral concept. First, it is unusual in that it may be used in a morally neutral descriptive sense (e.g., Copp tolerates his handicap—as a matter of fact), in a morally commendatory sense (e.g., Fest—properly—tolerates the

8

views of his colleagues), or in a morally negative sense (e.g., Fest—improperly—tolerates cheating in his classes).

Second, because the existence of toleration depends upon the existence of negative attitudes, tolerating will not be a feature of a utopian society.[4] One might imagine that a perfect society would have no need for generosity, because no one would be wanting; no need for retributive justice, because there should be no incidence of crime; and no need for tolerating, because we should have no occasion to develop negative attitudes.

The above two features combine to form a third. We cannot cogently develop a universal injunction to tolerate in the way we can a universal injunction to tell the truth or love one another. The reasons are, of course, that sometimes tolerating is morally wrong but also because the possibility of tolerating depends on the existence of certain negative attitudes, and not all people will possess them.

Tolerance

'Tolerance', as opposed to 'tolerating', may be either transitive or intransitive. We may say either that Banes is tolerant of Republicans (meaning that he has a particular attitude toward a particular group) or that Banes himself is a tolerant person (meaning, not primarily or necessarily that he has a tolerant attitude toward a great many things, but rather that tolerance is a feature of his character). Because tolerance has two distinct meanings, one having to do with an attitude and the other with a feature of character, we will discuss each separately.

Attitudinal tolerance does not seem to be related in any strict or clear-cut manner to one's actions. It is possible for a person to hold a tolerant attitude toward a particular act or practice and yet try to halt it.[5] We can imagine a police offi-

9

cer happening upon a group of teenagers who are smoking pot and saying: "Personally I have nothing against people smoking a little grass, though I don't believe it's a wise practice. However, your activity is against the law. I will have to confiscate your stuff and warn you not to do this again." Here, the officer has a tolerant attitude toward the teenagers' activity yet straightforwardly terminates their venture. On the other hand, it sounds strange to say that a person is tolerant of something and yet is doing everything possible to assist or advance it. If this is true, tolerance would also seem to require that we take little or no action to assist those things of which we are tolerant. One who actively and deliberately assists or nurtures the object of a favorable or neutral attitude is no longer tolerant of it but has come to accept it fully.

Attitudinal tolerance, then, differs from tolerating, although there may be overlap. Tolerating is the combination of a negative attitude toward something with the restraint from acting in accordance with that attitude. Tolerance, however, refers mainly to our attitudes. This difference between tolerating and tolerance yields another difference between the two concepts. Because tolerating is connected to action, it is easier to establish boundaries between tolerating and not-tolerating. People fail to tolerate when they take action of some sort to halt or impede those things that are the objects of their negative attitudes.

Even when it becomes increasingly difficult to tolerate something, however, we can often tell when people can no longer tolerate. There is no shading off between tolerating and not-tolerating: there is a sharp break. In the case of tolerance, however, we do not find this sort of distinctness. As Banes becomes increasingly tolerant, it often is difficult to say exactly when he is no longer merely tolerant but is something else. Similarly, as Grundy becomes increasingly less tolerant, it becomes increasingly difficult to say exactly when he fails to be tolerant at all.

10

But, if tolerance is primarily an attitude, what sort of attitude is it? We have said that tolerating entails a negative attitude. However, the attitudinal dimension relevant to the discussion of tolerance cannot be characterized simply as negative-neutral-positive. If we know that Banes is tolerant of Republicans, it is not actually clear whether he likes them, dislikes them, or is neutral with regard to them. Instead, the attitudinal dimension that seems relevant to tolerance ranges from total rejection, through passive acceptance, and finally all the way to wholehearted acceptance.

The question is whether an individual believes that something should not continue to exist, may—or has a right to—continue to exist, or whether its existence should be encouraged and nurtured. Grundy may believe that Republicans ought to be outlawed because they are a bane on society, but nevertheless he endures them because their activity is protected by law, he fears them, or whatever. If so, we would say that he tolerates Republicans but not that he is tolerant of them. On the other side, in the example of the police officer cited earlier, the officer is tolerant of the teenagers' activity in that he personally believes smoking marijuana is relatively harmless, but he does not tolerate it. Furthermore, being tolerant of something is compatible with having negative attitudes toward it. Imagine Webb saying, "I believe that smoking is a bad thing from a medical and an aesthetic perspective, but I nevertheless believe that people ought to be allowed to smoke if that is what they want to do." He is tolerant of smoking even though he clearly does not believe it is a good thing.

With tolerance, as in the case of tolerating, we can fail to be tolerant in either of two ways. First, we can fail by not endorsing the continued existence or value of something. When Grundy says, "Republicans ought to be bombed back into the Stone Age," he is not being tolerant of the GOP. Second, a person can fail to be tolerant of something by moving beyond

11

passive acceptance to a wholehearted embrace of it. When Banes, who until recently has been barely tolerant of Republicans, now proclaims that the GOP is the finest political party the nation has ever had, he has, we might say, transcended his tolerance of Republicans by coming to accept them fully.

When we turn to a description of tolerance as a feature of character, we have one or more of three things in mind. To begin with, those who are either habitually or from conviction normally tolerant of what they find in the world, who are quick neither to reject nor embrace what they find but give all its due, and generally find that most things in the world have something to be said for them—these are certainly tolerant people. David Hume comes to mind as one who viewed the world with such equanimity and who would be tolerant in this sense.[6] Let us term this first sort *habitual tolerance.*

This first type of tolerance, the calm acceptance of what one finds in the world, shades off into a second type, which might be characterized as judiciousness, fair-mindedness, or open-mindedness. Let us call this second sort *open-minded toleration.* It is closely allied with habitual tolerance but differs from it in that, while the habitually tolerant person may generally assume that everything has a due, a value, or merit, the open-minded one is prepared to find that, after looking at all sides of an issue, certain things may be found to lack any redeeming quality.

To be open-minded, in the sense of being tolerant, however, does not mean merely to be willing to examine all the evidence or to listen to all points of view.[7] Consider a sincere Nazi who shipped Jews off to concentration camps only after having patiently listened to arguments against such policies. We might call such a Nazi "fair" but hardly tolerant. Open-mindedness that is synonymous with tolerance would have to include being willing to entertain and respect the values and points of view of others as well as evidence and arguments. It is for this reason that it is inappropriate to think of a scrupulous and fair-minded judicial system as tolerant. We expect a judiciary to be fair and to examine the evidence, but we do not expect it to acknowledge values or points of view lying outside the framework of its laws and legal procedures. In this regard, we can formulate a distinction between the fairest possible judicial system and the classical tolerance found in the sort of liberalism espoused by John Stuart Mill. Mill's ideology is tolerant in being open to a variety of perspectives and values.[8] In this sense, it embodies open-minded toleration of a very thoroughgoing sort.

There remains a third sense of being tolerant as a feature of character, a sense not closely related to the first two. We often speak of institutions, societies, and nations as tolerant, yet it is not easy to see how they could be considered tolerant in either of the two senses described above. It is not clear, for example, how we can say, without lapsing into anthropomorphism, that a nation has a certain attitude or is open-minded. When we speak of Denmark as a tolerant country or of San Francisco as a tolerant city, we are not talking about kinds of attitudes found in these places or describing their states of mind. Rather, what we seem to have in mind is that a wide variety of activities, people, and ways of life are allowed to exist in these places without legal or social impediment. That is, we are talking not about attitudes but simply about legal and social behavior. We may think of this behavior as *laissez-faire toleration.*

The moral status of toleration as a feature of character, in the three senses described above, is somewhat amorphous. In the liberal culture of the United States, it usually would be taken as a compliment to describe a person or an institution as tolerant. However, if our analysis is correct, it is not completely clear that this should be so. It is not self-evidently apparent that it should be considered good for a society to allow many different types of behavior to take place. Neither is it self-evident that we should admire a person who normally

13

has an attitude of acceptance toward a great many things. Furthermore, if open-mindedness is not the same as fairness, it is not apparent that this should always be admired. It is only possible to see why these things should be thought virtuous when they are discussed in a context of certain assumptions, principles, and values. This is a discussion to which we will turn in later chapters.

Intolerance and Intoleration

In much the same way that the distinctions between tolerating, tolerant attitudes, and tolerant persons (or societies) can be drawn, so distinctions can be drawn on the negative side of the concept. A tolerant act can be matched with an intolerant one, a tolerant attitude with an intolerant one, and a tolerant person (or society) with an intolerant one. Unfortunately, the family of toleration concepts is incomplete in that the noun form opposite 'toleration' and the verb form opposite 'tolerate' are not found in our natural English language. We feel no great need to coin 'intolerate' although at times, as we will see, 'not tolerate' does not do what 'intolerate' would do for us were it introduced into our language. However, we find it convenient to introduce the noun 'intoleration' as opposed to 'toleration'. As we will use this word, it has more behavioral connotations than 'intolerance', which, corresponding with 'tolerance', has attitudinal connotations. Thus when we speak of intoleration, the major emphasis will be on the intolerant actions of those involved; while when we speak of intolerance, the greater emphasis will be on their intolerant attitudes. Of the two, we think of intoleration as the more generally applicable concept because (a) for several reasons we emphasize behavior more than attitudes in this study, and (b) exhibiting intolerant behavior connotes the presence of an intolerant attitude in more contexts than the reverse. We will have more to say about 'intoleration' in chapter 4.

It is misleading, then, to suppose that these concepts are matched completely except that there is forbearance and a softened attitude on the toleration side, whereas there is no forbearance and a tough negative attitude on the other side. In fact, one of the main claims of this study is that no easy understanding of any of these concepts follows from an understanding of its opposite. Chapter 4 on intoleration, in particular, will address the issue of the asymmetries between the positive and the negative sides of the toleration concepts. Still, for now, mention of one of these asymmetries is useful, if only as a cautionary reminder against making quick inferences about intoleration when toleration and the other positive toleration concepts are being discussed in chapters 2 and 3.

This asymmetry relates to the two ways that people can leave the arena of toleration. They can leave, as we have already noted, by becoming intolerant, or they may exit by coming to accept what they only tolerated in the past. Notice that these two doors out of toleration are not available for intoleration. This can be put paradoxically as follows: the more tolerant we become the less tolerant (i.e., the more accepting) we become. In contrast, increased intoleration simply leads to more of the same. There is, in short, only one door out of intoleration, and that is out the front door. Out that door, we either become tolerant or, as occasionally happens, we jump over toleration by directly accepting what we have hitherto rejected.

Roles of the Toleration Concepts

2

Clues about Roles

Our introductory look at the meaning of several of the toleration concepts fails to give us a full sense of their meanings not only because it is introductory but also because the question about the role these concepts play in our experiences has yet to be broached. In fact, as we shall see, these concepts play several unique roles for us. A clue about one of these roles was uncovered in the previous chapter when we observed that tolerating or being tolerant implies being permissive in disapproving fashion. More needs to be said about this feature of disapproval, in particular about how intense or mild it can be. Nonetheless, this clue about disapproval, along with other clues, suggests that one of toleration's several unique roles is to help us focus upon the limits of the behavior of others to which we are willing grudgingly to accede.

That this is a unique role can be appreciated, in part, by making comparisons with some of the more general evaluative concepts as they get expressed in our language. It can be argued that 'good' is also a kind of limiting word. That Albert is a good candidate for the job does not preclude saying that Burt is better and Charles is the best. So to say that Albert is good for the job can be a bit grudging or limiting, much as if the personnel director at the factory were to say, "Yes, Albert's all right," and then add, "however. . . ." Still, in most contexts, to say that someone or something is good is at least to register approval, other things being equal.

The same can be said about other very general evaluative

concepts or words such as 'just', 'ought', 'honorable', and 'moral', that have little or no descriptive meaning. All of them, more or less, can be used to register at least prima facie approval. Less general evaluative concepts with fairly specific descriptive meanings do similar jobs. To be classed as kindly, benevolent, thoughtful, helpful, honest, or trustworthy is also to receive approval rather than disapproval. In like fashion the opposites of these and some other concepts help us to register at least prima facie disapproval. With all of these concepts the presumption is that, other things being equal, the behavior that follows will correspond with our approval or disapproval, whichever is appropriate.

Thus, when persons call an instance of behavior good, we assume that they approve of it, and then, if they are sincere, we expect them to attempt to bring about that kind of behavior in themselves and/or others. Likewise, when they call behavior bad, we assume that they disapprove of it, and, sincerity presumed, we expect them to take steps to forgo that behavior in themselves as well as to keep others from engaging in it. In contrast, one of the unique features of tolerating and some of the other toleration concepts is a dissonance between approval/disapproval and behavior. At least a dissonance exists on the positive side. With intoleration the correspondence between disapproval and behavior is roughly as it is with the negative concepts alluded to above. To be intolerant of the noise someone is making is both to disapprove of it and to take steps to stop it. But with tolerating, because the disapproval is, so to speak, inept, a dissonance between disapproval and behavior occurs. As we shall see, this dissonance helps make it a limiting concept.

Although somewhat less unique, another feature of toleration that serves as a clue to its role in setting limits is that it is an agent/judge concept. In contrast, most evaluational concepts help us to evaluate not only agents/judges but all sorts of objects (e.g., paintings, cars, baseball players, schools) and acts. 'Good', 'just', 'honest', and 'beautiful' can all be used to evaluate objects and acts of various sorts. When so used, these words or concepts usually draw our attention away from the evaluator. What "That was a good thing to do" says about the speaker, it says by implication (e.g., that he/she has reasons for the evaluation and that approval is present). Even such indirect speech acts as "I believe that was the right thing to do" shift our attention away from the object only partially. With 'tolerating', the shift is more pronounced because references to the agent/judge are no longer optional. Grammatically the following form is mandatory:

(Pro)noun + Toleration + (X)

where X stands for the object of the toleration (and is optional in "He is tolerant") and the (pro)noun indicates that reference to the judge/agent is required. As will become evident shortly, this grammatical form is another clue about the role 'tolerating' plays in telling us that those who are tolerating are near the limit of what they can endure.

In order to get a more precise view of this role, one more clue about tolerating must be uncovered and put in place. This clue concerns the degree of intensity of the dissonance feature possessed by the concept of toleration. Notice how grudging someone's tolerating can be. Sheila can say of an unfortunate relationship between herself and a relative:

1. I tolerate him, but just barely!
2. I can hardly tolerate him!
3. He is almost intolerable!

In contrast, it hardly makes sense to talk about enthusiastic toleration. The closest we come to that is when we shift to the character aspect of toleration and describe a person as being habitually tolerant. But even here we usually have an image of this person putting up with a lot of abuse from others and

19

not particularly liking it. In this sense, being habitually tolerant is not the same as being easygoing, because the easygoing or laid-back person is someone who could not care less about what is going on and, therefore, cannot be said to be putting up with a lot of abuse. The responses or attitudes circumscribed by tolerating thus seem to range from near rebellion, on the one side, all the way to permanent resignation that lies just short of condoning, on the other.

The Tolerator

Actually it is somewhat misleading to speak of a role that a word has in a language or some part of a language, as was done in the previous section and in chapter 1. It is not words by themselves but speech acts[1] (or strings of speech acts)[2] containing words that play roles in a language. To speak of the role of 'tolerating' in our discourse is, most fundamentally, to speak of using that word in speech acts to make assertions of one sort or another. If this is right, and if, as speech-act theorists argue, we often cannot understand a speech act without taking account of who utters it, then the role of 'tolerating' in our language cannot be fully understood unless we take account of the various speakers who are likely to use 'tolerating', its cognates, or its various synonyms in speech acts.

These utterers or speakers include, among others, (a) those who tolerate (the tolerators), (b) those who are intolerant (the intolerators), (c) those who are not even tolerated (the intolerated), and (d) those who are tolerated (the tolerated). Focusing first upon the tolerators, the clues gathered so far suggest that the kinds of speech acts that these tolerators will often utter are warnings that they are close to the limit of what they can stand. It is true that in certain contexts when Sheila, who is tolerating, addresses an uninvolved observer on the scene with the words "I tolerate him and his ways," what is said may be primarily descriptive (assertive) in nature. But in those settings when Sheila is speaking to the tolerated person, or someone else who can intervene in one way or another in the situation, to say "I tolerate you (him) and your (his) ways" can indirectly be prescriptive (directive) with a force like that of the needle on an automobile tachometer registering in the yellow zone preceding the red-line area. In one sense the tachometer can also be thought of as playing a purely descriptive role in that it reads, let us say, 7,200 RPM. Yet the main role of the needle in the yellow zone is not to describe but to play the role of saying, "Back off on the accelerator; you have nearly reached the limit of what the engine can stand." Similarly, given the special feature that 'tolerating' has of focusing on the agent and of being adverbally modifiable with such borderline expressions as *barely* and *hardly*, tolerating speech acts are especially suited to play warning or limiting roles. Thus when Sheila says, "I tolerate you," as a warning, her intent is to have the effect of saying to the listener, "Don't push me anymore. Push a little more and I will cross the border into intolerance."

Just as there can be a struggle to maintain a tolerant composure, so there can be a struggle on the other side. Initially, it might seem otherwise because we often picture the intolerant person as rigid and self-righteous. But degrees of intolerance are evident in our talk of one person's being very intolerant and another being somewhat that way. The degrees of intolerance can, in fact, take us to the border or limit as is evident in such expressions as "I am trying to be tolerant (but failing, thank God)" and "I've almost gotten to the point of tolerating (standing) his ways".

It is even conceivable that speech acts of intoleration will also have a warning function to play. In these cases, of course, it will make no sense to say that the warning is aimed at the one who is hoping for toleration or eventually for total

21

acceptance. Joe, who is intolerant, cannot threaten by saying, "Look, if you push me, I'm going to tolerate you." Yet, given his state of borderline intoleration, he can say things to warn his allies. To announce to his allies that they have drifted near the border of toleration is to warn them to get away from that danger zone. Joe's admonitions here will take the form of "Let us be vigilant," "We are becoming overly permissive," "Little by little we are losing our standards," as well as "Be careful, lest we become tolerant (of these evils)." We will say more on cases of this type shortly.

The Intolerated

The roles of the tolerating words (speech acts) are also unique when viewed from the perspective of those who want to be tolerated (i.e., the intolerated) and their allies. These roles might not seem unique at first because "Don't be so intolerant," "Try to be tolerant," and "Try not to be so intolerant" would appear to be straightforward prescriptives (i.e., directives).[3] But compare "(Try to) be tolerant" with the following three prescriptives:

4. Love thy neighbor.
5. Vote Democrat.
6. Tell the truth.

There is a difference here because with "Be tolerant" what is being prescribed is basically passivity ("Let her be") whereas with 4, 5, and 6 the listener is being directed to do something. Also, by itself, "Be tolerant" does not specify what the behavior is of which someone is being asked to be tolerant. But, there is a more important difference. "Be tolerant" is a *minimal prescriptive* whereas 4, for example, is not. To put the matter roughly, when we are asked to love our neighbors, it is both our bodies and our souls that allegedly need changing. With "Be tolerant" it is only an alteration of our body's behavior that concerns the intolerated and their allies. That is, to love our neighbors requires adopting, it is tempting to say, a whole new ideology. We are being asked not only to do certain things but to do these things with a certain attitude, outlook, or orientation.

Much the same can be said of the injunction "Vote Democrat." It is voting that is being prescribed, but nothing in the prescription suggests or implies that the prescriber will be satisfied just with a vote. On the contrary, over and above that, what is most likely being urged upon us is support for the party, work for it, belief in its ideology, and the like.

Now with "Be tolerant" we are certainly being urged to passively accede to what others are or are not doing. And this acceding can be generalized in that if we ought to be tolerant in situation A, we ought also to be tolerant in situation B, which is like A. But although the acceding is generalizable, little else is. Those who are being asked to tolerate are not in addition expected to change, or at least radically change, their outlook toward those whom they presently do not tolerate. If you dislike noisy children, you need not dislike them any less in order to tolerate them. If you dislike homosexuals, you need not dislike them any less in order to tolerate them. And if you dislike Catholics, you need not dislike them any less in order to tolerate them either. Furthermore, in each case, if you become tolerant (or tolerate them), you need not think of yourself as committed to advocating that people raise noisy children, encourage homosexuals, or join the Catholic church. At least in one sense of tolerating, all you are doing is putting up with them, enduring them, or coping as best you can with what you may consider a bad situation.

So an important role of some of the toleration concepts from the point of view of the intolerated is to make it possible for them to issue minimal prescriptives, that is, prescriptives that allow them to urge others to change their behavior with-

23

out necessarily changing their attitudes. Undoubtedly, this role is particularly important in a pluralistic society where, because groups of people want to maintain their own ways, life-styles, attitudes, and integrity, toleration must become a way of life.

The Intolerator

From the perspective of intolerant persons, the request that they be tolerant may not seem minimal in nature. Although they are not expected to change their outlook, tolerating will still be difficult for them because it goes against the grain psychologically—in that they are expected to "act" in a way that will create a dissonance between their attitudes and their behavior.

Also, what appears a minimal request to those urging toleration may not seem minimal to intolerant persons for a closely related but different reason. It may go against the grain not just psychologically but socially as well. Tolerating often contributes to pluralizing a relationship, a family, a group, an institution, or even a whole social order. Thus, those who are intolerant may not only personally oppose pluralization, they may also oppose it because they believe that too much pluralization exists for the social order to function well or even to function at all.

Social status may also contribute to the discomfort of those who are urged to tolerate. If those who tolerate are in a position of power, discomfort will not likely be present. If Cash tolerates a certain kind of behavior among his employees, he can also be spoken of as allowing that behavior to take place. Allowing and granting permission are status concepts. Only those with elevated social status like Cash's can allow or grant permission to others; and, of course, those with privileged social status may allow things that they do not favor

24

(and thus be tolerant of them) or things they favor (and thus be neither tolerant nor intolerant). But although tolerating persons may be in a position of power, they often are not.

For these weak tolerators or potential tolerators, the situation is quite different from Cash's. If tolerating becomes burdensome to them, they may find that they have no return ticket to the other side. Indeed, those to whom they extend their toleration, generated as it is from no particular position of power, will likely view this tolerating as permanent. Cash's toleration is going to be viewed, in contrast, against the backdrop of his status. What he gives away to his employees he can take back, so that what he gives will likely be viewed more as a privilege. What weak persons give away through their tolerant behavior is likely to be viewed as a right granted to others. So again those tolerating are put in a difficult position. They may see themselves perhaps as wanting to be tolerant (i.e., cooperative), but they will feel that they are likely to be taken advantage of if they become so.

Fear of the slippery slope may also be present. If Sally tolerates homosexuals in her neighborhood, what other tolerating is going to be demanded of her? What if some of "them" move into her apartment building and initiate conversations with the neighbor's son? With her own son? Will she next be expected to be not just tolerant but to transcend toleration by practicing total acceptance? So although asking people to move from intoleration to toleration may seem like a minimal move to some, for many reasons it may seem like a major move to those who are intolerant.

The Tolerated

The role the toleration concepts play for those who are being tolerated has its own unique features. Before people are tolerated, and soon after, they may view these concepts in a

25

positive manner. Being tolerated is, after all, better than nothing. But once toleration comes, utterances such as "I don't want to be merely tolerated" and "I can't stand your tolerant attitude" may be heard. Such pejorative uses need to be contrasted with those that would be uttered by people who are satisfied with only being tolerated. Surely we all know a few such people. One group of these few is made up of those individualists who just want to be left alone but who, nevertheless, have a sufficiently large number of minor but irritating social vices that they sorely test our tolerance levels. Another group includes those few who want more than toleration but realistically expect nothing more because they have never had even toleration in the past. We can imagine immigrants who were persecuted in the Old Country but now live in a society that, at least grudgingly, lets them go about their business.

Yet, in large part, these people will be few in number. Because those who tolerate will be permissive disapprovingly, those who are tolerated will always live in fear of becoming intolerated. Transfers and borderline instability, it should be obvious by now, are such that the anxiety from which tolerated people suffer is perfectly understandable. But there is another reason tolerated people might want and even hope for more than toleration. They can want more because what more they want need not be a lot more. This assertion may seem false, inasmuch as the only alternative to toleration on the side of getting something more might appear to be total acceptance. However, there are alternatives lying between toleration and acceptance that need to be explored if the perspective of those who are tolerated is to be appreciated.

In this connection consider the case of Lin, a minority type, who moved into a homogeneous, majority neighborhood. When he first moved in, Lin and his family were simply not tolerated. His home and property were attacked, and he and his family were told in no uncertain terms that they were expected to move out. However, with the help of a few understanding neighbors and with the passage of time, the Lins gradually came to be tolerated. With the passage of still more time, the Lins found that the disapproving stares of the neighbors evolved into stares of indifference. The members of the neighborhood, busy as they were, came neither to disapprove nor approve of them. Now they simply ignore the Lins and treat them as if they were not there. "They don't bother us," say the neighbors, "and we don't bother them." It could be argued that this new reaction to the Lins is a form of toleration. Perhaps it could be called tolerant-like or something approaching condoning the Lins. Whatever it is called, it is clearly a less dangerous state of affairs for the Lins because they are no longer near the border separating toleration from intoleration. As a result, their presence is no longer a constant reminder to their neighbors of something that they can hardly stand. Because the Lins are no longer viewed with disapproval, the latent power of that attitude to push them across the border into intoleration no longer threatens them.

Of course, the Lins could hope for still more, because they could hope to be accepted into the community. However, such acceptance should not be confused with, for example, Alice's acceptance of Abel's religion when they get married. Acceptance is interestingly ambiguous in these two settings. Alice's acceptance is a matter of adopting Abel's religious ideology as her own. There are degrees of acceptance here but, in the extreme, Alice's acceptance represents a total denial of pluralism. In contrast, to accept the Lins into the community is not necessarily to accept the ideology they bring with them. What it involves, perhaps, is making them the objects of curiosity, amusement, and even of respect. Further, to accept them into the community involves treating them like other community members. If there are social events, they are invited to them; if it is customary to greet people when passing, they are greeted; if jobs are available, the Lins are treated like other applicants for the job; if the religious views of the

27

community are discussed, their views are discussed just like other people's. In short, they are given all the invitations, privileges, and rights extended to the rest of the community.

Again, as with being ignored, being accepted in the community could be called a form of toleration. If it were, it would probably be called the noble or ideal form of that concept by many. And indeed this form has been used, especially by some philosophers, in painting a portrait of the pluralistic society at its best.[4] However, there are two reasons for supposing that this is a peripheral use of that concept at best or at worst a stipulative use. First, and as already noted, the element of disapproval is no longer present in this use or at least is so diminished as to be absent for all practical purposes. Second, the passivity inherent in toleration is also diminished significantly. In the paradigm cases, one is tolerant or tolerates by passively permitting those who are tolerated to do as they wish. It is even part of this passive portrait of those who are tolerating to imagine them suppressing a grumble or two and certainly not giving any aid or comfort to those they tolerate. But with "noble" toleration we might see the Lins' neighbors, for example, not only making the Lins feel welcome in the community but even making contributions, and willingly so, to their church or temple. Although the members of the community do not in fact join the Lins' religious group, and thus in this sense passively allow them to practice their religion, they give that religion enough aid and comfort that the use of 'toleration' in this setting begins to feel somewhat inappropriate.

In addition, then, to being just tolerated, the tolerated person could hope to be ignored (i.e., condoned, in one sense of the meaning of that word) or even accepted by others in the community. Thus there is no mystery why, from the tolerated person's point of view, toleration can become a pejorative concept.

28

Other Uses

Up to this point the focus of attention in understanding the roles toleration concepts play in our language has been upon the different speakers or users of these concepts, namely, the tolerators, the intolerators, the intolerated, and the tolerated. In order to get a broader sense of how people use toleration concepts, it is necessary to focus attention upon the hearers as well. Tolerators do not just warn those they tolerate. They also commiserate with other tolerators, criticize those who are intolerant, and also extend sympathy to those who are not tolerated. Similarly, those who would like to be tolerated (the intolerated) not only urge the intolerant to tolerate them but also encourage others of their kind to support their cause, praise those who tolerate, and perhaps express envy for those who are tolerated. Many combinations of speech are obviously possible. Further, a speaker can say more than one kind of thing to a hearer. So the uses identified in this chapter represent only a selection of the more interesting kinds rather than the complete set of combinations that people may employ when they talk to one another about tolerating and toleration.

It should also be clear, and some of the examples cited suggest as much, that these ways of speaking or using toleration concepts are not restricted to cases where the speakers and hearers are individuals. Individuals can tolerate individuals or groups, and groups can tolerate other groups or individuals. Although groups are made up of individuals, it makes sense to think of those people acting as a group and thereby being tolerant or intolerant as a group, or being the recipient as a group of toleration or intoleration from others. Of these combinations, there might be some doubt about individuals tolerating very large groups or institutions. Can one lonely person tolerate the government? Can one lowly private be intolerant of an army? Generally the answer is yes. Large institutions can be tolerated or not tolerated provided someone is in position to respond to them, even if only verbally. We may not be able by our individual efforts to take a swipe at government that is powerful enough to force it to submit to our will. However, as we have suggested in chapter 1, so long as we are able in some way to respond, and actually do so, we can be said to be intolerant. Likewise, so long as we refrain from responding, we can also meaningfully be said to tolerate.

Toleration & Reason Giving

3

Appropriateness of Reasons

People who tolerate cannot always give, or do not always have, reasons for tolerating because they may have come to their tolerating out of habits whose origins are unknown to them. Both in the behavioral sense in which we say we tolerate someone and in the more attitudinal sense of that concept when we say we are tolerant, it is possible to lack reasons for tolerating or even to be unaware of the tolerating state itself. Toleration is not strictly a conscious-state concept in the way intention and pain are.

Nonetheless, although we may in certain settings be unable to give reasons for tolerating or being tolerant, when we advocate toleration, reasons are required. In part this is because advocacy generally is reason demanding. We do not baldly say, "You ought to do this" without presupposing that reasons can be given to justify our prescriptions. Of course, in certain circumstances (e.g., those requiring military secrecy) the reasons may not actually be forthcoming. But the reasons need to be available; we do not linguistically tolerate someone who says, "You ought to do this but I have no reasons for saying so."

Yet over and above this general demand for reasons, the concept of toleration has its own special need to collect reasons simply because it goes against the grain to tolerate. As we have already observed, to tolerate is to act (or fail to act) in one way while at the same time being inclined to act in another. Mary wants to tell Joe to put out his cigar but refrains from doing so because she fears he will leave her if she does.

31

Because our inclination in these kinds of situations is to speak up, we have a built-in reason for not tolerating. It seems that those who urge toleration have one strike against them.

If the reasons for tolerating have to be especially good to overcome an inherent bias against toleration, it is especially important to have a sense of how good one's reasons are for tolerating. However, it makes little sense to attempt to assess the adequacy of the particular reasons given in a particular setting without having some overall sense for the kinds of reasons that can be provided to justify toleration and, second, for assessing how these kinds of reasons relate to one another.

Methodological-Procedural Reasons

Consider the following three similar examples of reason giving.

1. I urge you to be patient (tolerant) until we get an explanation (more information, data).
2. I'm trying to be tolerant, as it will give everyone a chance to cool down (and think more clearly later).
3. We must tolerate other people's points of view because, in the long run, truth (or creativity, self-expression, diversity) will be maximized if we do.

What these examples have in common is that their reasons are all, loosely speaking, methodological or procedural in nature. They all commend toleration to us on grounds that certain methods or procedures need to be applied. In 1 and 2 toleration is urged upon us so that other things may happen. The toleration in these cases is a kind of temporary suspension of judgment and activity. Presumably, once the period of suspension is over, it is open for us to tolerate or not, because we no longer can be faulted for having prejudged the issue at hand.

32

Number 3 is similar to 1 and 2 in that toleration helps other things happen. Yet it differs in urging permanent rather than temporary toleration. It differs further in not urging a total suspense of judgment the way 1 and 2 do. With the latter two, we are not supposed to make any judgment, especially inasmuch as the speaker suspects that we have a natural inclination to intolerantly jump to conclusions. With 3 those who are urged to be tolerant are not being asked to give up or suspend whatever views they hold. Rather, they are being asked to suspend final judgment only. Or, to put it differently, they are being asked to keep an open mind over the long haul while still holding a point of view on various issues.

Now consider the following example.

4. We should all be tolerant of each other's (moral) views because, in the end, none of us can prove that his/her position is the correct one.

Number 4 is like 3, and unlike 1 and 2, in urging permanent toleration. Yet it differs from 3 radically in other respects. With 4, toleration does not yield anything for us. It does not gain us time so that we may think more, gather more data, cool down, or gain perspective. In fact, it does just the opposite. It represents a state at which we are supposed to arrive after we have rationally done all we can. It is not that we are being asked to apply a procedure and, perhaps as a part of doing so, to be tolerant. Rather, because the procedure we normally rely on has failed, we are told we ought to suspend our judgment permanently.

It is instructive to contrast 4 with 5.

5. We should not tolerate this behavior because we all know right from wrong, and this behavior is wrong.

This is an utterance of a dogmatist instead of a skeptic, and in this case what is being preached is intoleration rather than toleration. However, logic does not demand this response. The behavior that concerns the dogmatist may be wrong in and of itself; but other (moral) considerations may override its presumed wrongness, so that it is still logically open for the speaker to preach or practice toleration. This kind of reason giving, in which a lesser evil is chosen in order to avoid a greater evil, is one of the most important when applying the concept of toleration, as we shall see shortly. But this form aside, a variation of 5 shows, in another way, that the dogmatist is not logically bound to the concept of intoleration.

> 5a. We know right from wrong, and what we know is that being tolerant is right in this situation.

If dogmatism were tied to intoleration, 5a would be self-contradictory. But it is not. Although 5a does not reveal how we know that toleration is right, it presupposes in its use of *know* that we have applied rational methods to justify our saying that we should be tolerant in a specific situation. It is true that we might inadvertently misapply our method, or we may be faking; but because 5a is meaningful, dogmatism is clearly no more logically tied to intoleration than is skepticism to toleration.

Still, a feeling exists that skepticism and toleration on the one side, and dogmatism and intoleration on the other, are tied together if not logically (i.e., necessarily) then in some other way. In part the seeming tie may result from confusing items like 1 and 2 with those like 4. With 1 and 2, the toleration is nearly reduced to a form of irritated patience. We not so patiently wait, and either the patience itself, or other things that get done while we are patient, puts us in a better position to render a judgment of whether we should be permanently tolerant or not. Yet superficially, the lack of information and perspective as expressed in 1 and 2 resembles the deficiency of information and perspective expressed in 4. The two are similar enough that it might seem reasonable to accept 4 because it is reasonable to accept 1 and 2. But it is reasonable to accept 1 and 2 because the lack of information and perspective is correctable. Inasmuch as these deficiencies cannot be corrected in 4, the toleration recommended in 4 needs some further justification if it is to be accepted.

Another reason 4 sounds plausible is because it can also be confused with sentences like 4a.

> 4a. We ought to be tolerant about each other's views on abortion because, after all, there is no way to prove that our views are right or wrong on this single issue (because my view depends upon the existence of the immortal soul, and yours does not).

With 4a as against 4, only one issue is not amenable to proof or at least generates disagreement among those involved in the discussion. On other issues, let us assume, all those involved share common ethical and political views. Evidently, 4a has application in part because of the intractable lack of knowledge that plagues the issue of abortion. But more than the matter of a lack of knowledge separates 4a from 4; 4a may also be concerned with protecting the status quo regarding the participants' common ethical and political base. If that is so, a paraphrase of 4a would be: "Let us be tolerant on this issue because: (a) otherwise it may come to divide us generally, and (b) we can't be sure who is right." Thus, toleration is reasonable with 4a, where the lack of knowledge is intractable but limited in scope, and other important concerns may be at stake. In contrast, when the lack of knowledge is both intractable and unlimited (as in 4), it is difficult to see what sense it makes to favor toleration over intoleration. It could just as well be argued that we should practice intoleration "because, in the end, none of us can prove that his/her position is the correct one." It is tempting to be skeptical here because rampant skepticism can be used to justify toleration—or intoleration for that matter.

Tactical-Empirical Reasons

Consider next the following example of reason giving.

> 6. Let us be tolerant. They will soon tire and get bored with what they are doing (and shortly desist as a result).

If the senses of toleration in 1 and 2, and possibly 3, above can best be characterized as methodological, 6 is best characterized as tactical (-empirical). Here there is no question of any form of suspense of judgment. The speaker knows full well what the situation is and has no immediate intention of weighing things and possibly changing his or her mind about anything. Instead, the speaker advocates a temporary form of toleration because he or she figures (empirically) that in the long term this tactic will lead to certain desired results for his or her group. And what the group wants does not involve a change in behavior on its part but on the part of those whom it is temporarily tolerating. Contrast 6 with 6a, which could easily be confused with it.

> 6a. Let us be tolerant. Once they appreciate our tolerant reaction to their provocations, they will become embarrassed and soon desist.

Here again those tolerated are expected to change, but now they do so directly as the result of the toleration that is being exhibited rather than as the result of the passing of time and the performance of certain acts that accompany the toleration (as in 6).

Both 6 and 6a can be contrasted to 7.

> 7. I tolerate his ways for now because I figure that I will

36

adjust to them soon, and they will no longer bother me.

This form of toleration is also tactical (-empirical); only now the tactics are supposed to work on the one who tolerates rather than on the tolerated. The change in this particular form of toleration is quite different from that form found in 1, 2, and even 3, where those who tolerate do so by suspending judgment in one form or another. In these examples toleration is followed by judgments whose results are completely unpredictable. After all, we suspended judgment in order to be open to new solutions for problems that are bothering us. So once the suspense-of-judgment form of toleration is over, it is possible to move into a new form of toleration, to intoleration, or to some other state of behavior or attitude. With 7, in contrast, the toleration leads to predictable results. The speaker expects to move beyond toleration to some form of acceptance. Here, instead of suspending judgment, the speaker is making a judgment to suspend all behavioral responses until his or her emotions, attitudes, and the like get in line with those of the person tolerated.

A kind of hybrid instance of the methodological and tactical forms of toleration is exhibited in 8.

> 8. I put up with him (my husband) in this regard because I do not know how he would react if I didn't. He might commit suicide, go berserk, attack me—who knows?

One reason this example counts as a mixed case is that it is not clear whether the wife is going to take any steps to deal with the unknown in the way she clearly would if she were practicing methodological toleration. Further, the unknown in 8 is not completely unknown. Although the speaker does not know what the person being tolerating will do, she knows enough to sense that whatever is likely to happen will not be good.

Personal-Prudential Reason Giving

Number 8 suggests a series of other examples where the person doing the tolerating knows full well what will happen if toleration is not the order of the day.

> 9. I put up with her (my wife's) ways because I am tired of nagging, fighting, and arguing (i.e., little or nothing will happen).
> 10. I put up with him (I tolerate his ways) because I am afraid of what he would do to me (e.g., beat me, leave me) if I didn't.
> 11. I (Slim) tolerate Sam because there is not much else I can do.

These personal-prudential examples differ from those where tactical reason giving is taking place in several respects. To be sure, with 9 an aspect of tactical reason giving remains present. The tactics are that, if the speaker tolerates, he can avoid the fatigue that accompanies fighting, nagging, and the like. But even here the tactics, if that is what they should be called, are different from those in examples 6–8. With these cases, the tactics employed are designed to bring about some hoped-for and empirically expected change in the situation. Either those who tolerate or those tolerated are expected to undergo some sort of transformation. That hardly is the case with 9. It is probably best characterized as reason giving that expresses a fixed personal policy based upon a full empirical awareness of the situation. The husband in 9 could choose to nag and fight and perhaps do other things as well (e.g., leave the arena of tolerating completely) but chooses not to do so. What is tolerated here, it has been decided, is personally less painful than the hassling. It is as if he believes that the cure is worse than the disease.

With 10, it is not the effort that is worse than the disease.

Rather one disease (i.e., what is tolerated) is perceived as less serious than another (i.e., the pain of not tolerating). With 9, the one tolerated (the wife) passively resists and wins in the end by stubbornly continuing her ways. In contrast, the tolerated person in 10 (the husband) actively blocks the desire not to tolerate with threats and even occasional applications of force.

The coercive elements in 10, but more so in 11, raise a difficult issue. A hint of this issue occurs even in 9. The issue, discussed to some extent in chapters 1 and 2, has to do with tolerating a situation over which one has little or no control. In 9, the hint is that the nagging and fighting is of no use, and tolerating is about all that can be done. In 10, the coercion is so heavy that the tolerating looks good by contrast. In 11, Slim admits openly that nothing much can be done. Does this admission turn 11, and possibly 10 as well, into deviant cases? If people have no choice, how can they be said to tolerate in any sense of that word? Indeed, it makes no sense for Slim to say that he tolerates Sam behaviorally if Sam is much stronger than Slim and Sam is always willing to employ force to get his way.

However, the toleration concepts have many senses, and some have application even in those settings where a person cannot control the physical environment. If Slim cannot physically do anything about Sam's smoking and knuckle cracking, he can at least complain about it and in that way exhibit his negative reaction. Conversely, he can tolerate by remaining silent. But if Slim is not even permitted to speak up without being brutalized, he can still control his attitudes toward what is happening to him by stoically accepting the inevitable. He can still disapprove of Sam's behavior, but he need no longer rage internally at what he physically cannot alter. The toleration concepts (more particularly 'tolerant' rather than 'tolerate') thus have application even in cases like 10 and 11. They seem deviant only when we fail to realize how varied they are and when we therefore fail to notice that, even if they cannot be applied in a particular situation for one reason, they might be applicable in another situation for another reason.

Normative Reason Giving

The following cluster of examples moves the reason giving in a radically new direction. Although 12 below represents perhaps a transition between the previous cluster and this one, the remainder draw our attention to normative reasons in a way that the previous examples have not.

12. I tolerate because I don't want to fight—I don't fight.
13. I tolerate him because I feel sorry for him (and we ought to feel pity, etc., for our fellow humans).
14. We must (learn to) be tolerant of them, because they do not actually do much harm.
15. We should be tolerant because all of us have a right to pursue our own life-styles.
16. I try to be tolerant because tolerance is a virtue.[1]

In all these examples, either explicitly or implicitly, goods are being chosen over other goods (e.g., with 16 we forsake the satisfactions of giving rein to our attitudes in order to achieve a valued state of character, and with 15 we forgo the pleasure and benefits of having things go our way in favor of the rights of others) or one evil over another (e.g., as in 14 where the evil of interfering is not chosen thus allowing others to continue their small harms). It is simply the nature of these reason-giving examples to involve a comparison of values.

Actually all other tolerating examples involve comparisons as well. Procedural examples compare the advantages of acting now (i.e., the joys of intoleration) against those of acting later (i.e., the decrease of ignorance in the decision-making process). In the tactical-empirical cases, toleration helps to eliminate the less preferred of two states in a context in which the tacticians think they know as a matter of fact what will happen if they tolerate or decide not to. With the personal-prudential forms of toleration, the comparison is between two personal states.

In contrast, the purest type of normative toleration features the comparison of at least two normative states: moral, aesthetic, or whatever. With less pure types, normative toleration can be combined with other types, as with 3.

3. We must tolerate other people's points of view because, in the long run, truth (or creativity, self-expression, diversity) will be maximized, if we do.

In this example the comparison is between the enjoyment and benefit of possessing the truth and the enjoyment of viewing other peoples' ideas with disgust and disdain. Toleration here entails forgoing the latter enjoyment in hope of attaining the truth in the future. Number 3 is not a clear-cut example of normative toleration, however, because the ideal of possessing the truth is open ended. We do not know what the truth we seek will be, but we still value it. So 3 also looks a bit like an example of procedural or methodological toleration.

Summary

Granting that some examples, like 3, will overlap with others, it remains possible to distinguish four basic types of toleration.

1. *Procedural-methodological toleration.* The purpose of this form of toleration is to help those who tolerate gain insights—to go from the unknown to the known. This toleration is temporary, brings about change

mainly in the one who tolerates, is behavioral in nature, consequentialist, and extensive (i.e., it is greater rather than lesser because in most examples of this form of toleration judgments are suspended completely). This form of toleration is applicable both to individuals and to groups, both to those who tolerate and to those who are tolerated.

2. *Tactical-empirical toleration.* The purpose of this form of toleration is to bring about a change to a state that is known and predictable. Of necessity this form is temporary, behavioral, consequentialist, varying in degree (but probably greater than lesser in degree), and applicable both to individuals and to groups (in that those employing the tactics can be individuals or groups and those tolerated can be individuals or groups).

3. *Personal-prudential toleration.* The purpose of this form is to reflect settled personal preferences via prudential calculations already reached. This form of toleration tends to be permanent but may or may not be consequentialist. It is primarily behavioral (but not infrequently is attitudinal) and can be greater or lesser in degree. In addition it can be applied, especially in its prudential form, to groups as well as to individuals.

4. *Normative toleration.* The purpose of this form of toleration is to reflect tolerating judgments or preferences. Because these judgments are settled, they tend to be permanent. They are also behavioral and can apply to individuals or groups.

In addition to the four basic types of toleration, a series of characteristics or dimensions can be identified that attach to all or most of the four basic types.

A. *Temporary* (e.g., most procedural and tactical forms of toleration) *vs. permanent* (e.g., normative toleration based on rights, especially as in "We should be tolerant because, after all, each of us has a right to speak freely") *toleration*. Within this group on the temporary side there can be:

1. A change in the one (those) tolerating (e.g., "We should tolerate for now, because I'm sure we'll get used to their ways") *vs.* a change in the one (those) tolerated (e.g., "If we're tolerant now, they will settle down and not raise quite so much fuss").

2. A change in which the toleration is the reason for the change (e.g., "Our tolerant behavior will set an example for them and they will, as a result, change their ways") *vs.* a change where the toleration is only the cause or only a condition that permits the change to take place (e.g., "If we are tolerant, we will have time to gain some perspective on this issue and decide how to deal with it later").

B. *Consequential vs. nonconsequential toleration.* Within this group on the consequential side there can be predictable (e.g., as in tactical) toleration *vs.* unpredictable (e.g., as in procedural toleration) consequences.

C. *Attitudinal* (e.g., "I am not bothered the way I used to be by the way they do things in the Army; I have learned to be tolerant") *vs. behavioral* (e.g., "I tolerate his heavy drinking, but what I'd really like to do is kick his . . .") *toleration*.

D. *Greater* (e.g., "He is a very tolerant person" or "I have no real trouble putting up with his peculiar ways") *vs. lesser* (e.g., "I can hardly stand him") *toleration*.

E. *Individual vs. group toleration.* Various combinations occur here. Individuals can tolerate groups, groups can tolerate individuals, groups can tolerate other groups, and individuals can tolerate other individuals. Within this kind of toleration there can be:

1. Toleration of and by individuals in a group (e.g., Catholics tolerating small groups of Protestants living in the neighborhood) *vs.* toleration of and by

43

groups (institutions) themselves (e.g., the Catholic church tolerating the presence of Eastern Orthodox churches in a predominantly Catholic country).

2. Toleration internal to the group (e.g., "We tolerate some diversity within the order") *vs.* toleration external to the group (e.g., "We tolerate other faiths").

Intoleration & Reason Giving

Parallels

Our study of the reasons given for tolerance can teach us much about reasons given for intolerance. Normative reasons, for example, are roughly as appropriate for those who do not bend a little as for those who do, as is evident below with 1, 2, and 3.

1. We must be intolerant of this sort of behavior (cheating, loose talk by servicemen in time of war, terrorism, strikes) because it is wrong (immoral).
2. We cannot permit anyone to deprive anyone else of his or her right to speak.
3. It is my responsibility as the foreman of this shop to see that pilfering of supplies stops. We cannot tolerate this sort of behavior.

The primary difference between these cases and the normative reasons given in the previous chapter is that a shift has taken place in our view of whose interests are most weighty. When we tolerate, the interests of those who are tolerated usually count for more. They are doing something wrong, but we still refrain from acting against them because we value their right to act, their well-being, and so forth more highly than the good we would achieve by restraining them. Or perhaps we tolerate them because they are more powerful than we. In contrast, with intoleration, our interests, the interests of some third party, or even the "real" interests of the one we do not tolerate usually get priority. It may be important to consider Sam's right to speak out on every issue, but when he

45

blurts out military secrets, and thereby endangers other people's lives, we may want to override his right to speak.

Personal-prudential reason giving is also appropriate when someone is acting intolerantly.

    4. I don't feel like tolerating. I am going to put an end to that foolishness. Why shouldn't I?
    5. Put out your cigar. I hate (am allergic to) smoke.

As against normative intoleration (and toleration) this form draws our attention to the interests of the one responding to certain forms of behavior, at least insofar as reasons are concerned (i.e., it is on balance this person's interests that lead to intoleration or toleration). But again, as with normative reason giving, personal-prudential reason giving on behalf of intoleration does not run completely parallel to the reason giving done on behalf of toleration. On the tolerating side, a balancing act of some sort is inevitable. Harry tolerates Sam's cigar smoking and thereby forgoes the pleasures of clean air for the sake of preserving their profitable business relationship. With intoleration, the same sort of balancing act is present in many, and perhaps most, cases, but it is not inevitable. It is present when Harry intolerantly finally tells Sam to snuff out his cigar, knowing full well that in so doing he will terminate their business relationship. But in other cases it is not a matter of balancing a good against a bad factor. Cash may simply be intolerant of an employee's cigar smoking because he hates the smoke. From his point of view the intolerant act of forbidding cigar smoking represents a pure-win situation because he now breathes odorless air and loses nothing except an easily replaceable employee. Surely it is these pure-win cases that help make many intolerant acts much sweeter than the tolerant ones.

    The parallel of tactical intoleration with tactical toleration is great but again not complete. With tactical toleration, it will be recalled, we tolerate in order to help bring about a predictable effect either in others (e.g., "They'll tire after awhile, and then we won't have to tolerate") or ourselves (e.g., "If we tolerate now, we'll get used to it so it won't bother us at all in the end"). With tactical intoleration, the means are different but the end result is predictably the same.

6. We must crack down on them and teach them a lesson. In the end they will desist.
7. Things will get worse unless we do something. We can't afford to be tolerant.

In both 6 and 7, where the tactics of intoleration are designed to work on others, the parallel with toleration is close. In contrast, examples of tactical intoleration where the tactics are being applied to oneself are hard to come by—although 8 below is, perhaps, a rare example.

8. We need to be intolerant for a while at least, so that we can prepare ourselves (for tolerating later).

In effect, 8 asks for a respite against what is viewed as an unavoidable and unfortunate condition.

Give or take a little, then, reason giving on the intoleration side is like that on the toleration side for three of the four types of reason giving identified in the previous chapter. The parallel holds with procedural reason giving as well. Recall that procedural toleration is a temporary state whose purpose is to allow time to gather data, settle down, and think through issues so that, in the end, a decision can be made as to how to act. The decision might eventually lead to tolerating behavior of a different form, to some form of intoleration, or to acceptance. Just as it is possible to tolerate a certain state of affairs while the data gathering proceeds, so it is possible to be intolerant while gathering data. The kinds of cases that come to mind are like 9 where people are intolerant because they suspect in advance of their research efforts that some danger is afoot.

9. We must halt the use of this chemical until the research shows us that it is not harmful to the environment.

The choice between procedural toleration and procedural intoleration in these kinds of cases appears at first glance to be made mainly by comparing gains and losses. Actually, the comparison is less concerned with gains versus losses than it is with losses versus losses, for we would hardly call 10 below a matter of tolerating.

10. While we perform research into the size of our profits, we will continue pumping oil out of these wells.

Number 10 is not a matter of tolerating because no negative factor is present. Notice how 10 differs with 11 in this regard.

11. Our workers must continue to put up with that noise but, in the meantime, we will conduct tests to see how much it affects production.

So opting either for toleration or intoleration in the procedural sense of these words is primarily a matter of estimating losses. If the preliminary assessment is that the losses will be marginal, procedural toleration would normally be in order; if the losses figure to be great, then procedural intoleration would normally be in order.

The parallel between the reason giving on the toleration and the intoleration sides holds up even in the face of a distinction between procedural intoleration and an intoleration of procedures. The former, as we have just seen, involves being intolerant of something (other than the procedures) while the procedures are being implemented. Intoleration of procedures, in contrast, involves refusal to employ data gathering and other rational procedures because, often, someone has something to hide. Here we quite naturally think of crooked politicians who are powerful enough to suppress investigations into their own or their friends' alleged wrongdoing, or of journal editors who refuse even to look seriously at, let alone publish, articles that threaten their own pet theories. We can also imagine more justifiable examples of the intoleration of procedures as, for example, during war when military commanders do not allow government agencies to test thoroughly new weapons that are urgently needed in the field. Yet in parallel fashion, just as there are unjustifiable and justifiable examples of the intoleration of procedures, so there are unjustifiable and justifiable examples of what might be called toleration of procedures. In connection with the latter, we are all familiar with the government commission that endlessly and expensively studies a problem and, as a result, manages to do nothing about it. Such examples of excessive toleration can be contrasted with examples where there is a need for study, and the study is done even though it is costly in time and effort.

Not-Tolerating

The scope of the reason giving that works against toleration cannot be fully understood by concentrating on *intoleration* or *intolerance*. The reason is that the contradictory of tolerating is not *intolerating* but *not-tolerating*, and not-tolerating is an ambiguous concept. If Sally says, "I can no longer tolerate this behavior," and she follows through on what she says, she has an option available to her. She can practice intoleration by attempting to restrain the offender in one way or another. Or she can retire or retreat from the scene. Notice how we speak about these matters. When Sally resigns her public office because she disapproves of the state's death penalty policies and then quietly moves on to take some position in business, it seems strained to call her intolerant of the state's policies. To be sure she cannot tolerate them, and because she cannot, she might very well express herself in one of the following ways.

12. I could not stand it any longer.
13. I could not tolerate such policies.
14. I cannot tolerate (stand, put up with) this any longer.

Not putting her response in terms of intoleration allows for the possibility, and even suggests, that active opposition to the death penalty is not what Sally has in mind. If, instead of simply resigning, she also began a public campaign against the death penalty, it would be quite natural for her to say things like the following.

15. We must not tolerate this way of dealing with criminals.
16. We must be intolerant of this deliberate killing of one human being by another—even when it is sanctioned by the judiciary and the legislature.

Actually our language is quite flexible here. It seems to reserve 'intolerant', 'intolerance', and 'intolerable' for those cases where the speaker actively opposes the behavior in question. Yet the English language has other devices for performing the same job. *Must* as used in 15 suggests active opposition rather than withdrawal or resignation. It also seems natural to shift to impersonal modes of speech (*"This* behavior cannot be tolerated") and to *we* (as against *I*) when active opposition is being pursued or contemplated. In contrast, first person, singular pronouns are especially appropriate when withdrawal is in order. It is as if *I* is more at home, as we might expect, with prudential and personal reason giving, where withdrawal is quite common. So also are expressions such as "can't stand" (as in "I—personally—can't stand him"), "can't abide," or "find it difficult to put up with him."

At least one other form of opposition to toleration needs to be considered. So far two forms, restraint (of the one offending) and retreat (of the offended person), have been identified. A third form is found in the following scenarios.

17. As far as Margaret is concerned, Alex's only fault as a husband is his cigar smoking. She strongly dislikes the smoke and smell of all cigars and, as a result, has been wondering what to do about her situation. She has done the best she can to tolerate but now finds that she can no longer do so. She has considered leaving Alex but has rejected this option, at least for the present, as too extreme. Other possibilities that occur to her are nagging Alex until he submits to her will or banishing him to the other bedroom. However, clever woman that she is, Margaret thinks up another possibility. Knowing that Alex's love for fried chicken is greater than his love for cigars, she makes him an offer. She promises that if he gives up cigar smoking she will prepare fried chicken for him, not once each week as is her custom, but every other day. Unable to resist such an offer, Alex gives up his cigars and they live happily ever after.

18. Nation X has a record of abusing the civil rights of certain minorities within its boundaries. Nation Y offers X much-needed economic aid, provided it will change its ways. X accepts Y's offer and, as a result, a situation that Y considers immoral is changed permanently for the better.

19. Harry can't stand his wife any longer. He considers shooting her but decides it is too messy. Instead he buys her off with a six-million-dollar settlement and leaves the scene a free man.

Clearly these scenarios show that it is possible to respond positively to intolerable situations. It is true that when we speak of an action as intolerant, we exclude the possibility of calling it a positive response. An intolerant act is one that involves coercion or a threat of coercion to stop (or start) somebody's untoward action (or inaction). But when we are speaking about a situation, rather than the response to it, words like *intolerable*, or more likely *not tolerable*, still leave open the possibility of a positive response, as with 17 and 18, and possibly 19, above.

Actually, our English language is a bit awkward when used to talk about positive responses to intolerable situations. In none of the above scenarios does it seem right to characterize the response as intolerant. Nor are we completely comfortable with "not a tolerant response." We are moved to give credit to those who are acting positively by using less negative-sounding expressions. Yet lacking an appropriate way of speaking, we back off and talk instead about the intolerant situation or at other times about the attitude of the one who can no longer tolerate. Notice in this connection how loosely we can talk about Margaret's change of attitude. That change enables us and her to say that something must be done about her situation. But having said that she has an intolerant attitude, or better yet one that no longer enables her to tolerate, does not exclude her option of a positive response.

Talk about people's attitudes is loose enough, in fact, to enable us to perform a variety of linguistic tasks with it. Consider 17 if Alex were to refuse Margaret's offer. What would it now mean to say that Margaret's attitude has become increasingly intolerant? More than likely it would mean that although she has not as yet acted intolerantly, she will do so shortly. If, however, she cannot act intolerantly because of Alex's strength and bad temper, then to say that she has an intolerant attitude means that she would act intolerantly if she could. In all of these uses, and others as well, talk about attitudes gives us the flexibility we lose when we concentrate our thinking on actions instead.

Although there are three basically different types of responses to situations where we can no longer tolerate, and many different ways to talk about them, it should not be assumed that it is always easy to sort these responses into one or another basic type. Margaret's fried chicken option is clearly a positive-type response. Just as clearly, punishing a child who has misbehaved is an intolerant (negative or restraining)-type response, and leaving the room in order to avoid loud music is a nontolerating (or retreating)-type response. However, is the response in 19 best classified as positive or retreating? It seems to involve a bit of both because Harry rewards his wife, but he does so in order to leave the marriage.

In a somewhat different vein, how are the responses to behavior that cannot be tolerated best classified in 20?

20. In Nation W no one is punished, overtly coerced, or directly threatened into behaving in accordance with its norms. Instead, when people exhibit deviant behavior, the environment that surrounds them is arranged so that they are positively reinforced to act normally again.

Certainly Nation W's responses to behavior it feels it cannot tolerate are not negative the way imprisonment, torture, and execution are. Because they are not negative, we are not so tempted as we might otherwise be to call them intolerant. Indeed they are designed to be positively reinforcing, that is, to reward normal or acceptable behavior. Nonetheless, inasmuch as the environment is arranged so that the person exhibiting deviant behavior does not choose conformity, but is instead conditioned to it, it is tempting to call W's policies intolerant after all.

Commendatory and Pejorative Concepts

It should be even more clear now why tolerance, tolerating, and so forth are not always commendatory and intolerance (etc.) not always pejorative concepts. Because reasons can be given to support either side, it will make sense, given the appropriate setting, to say any one of the following things without contradiction.

21. You ought to be tolerant.
22. You ought not to be tolerant.
23. You ought to be intolerant.
24. You ought not to be intolerant.

Those who tolerate are not always on the side of angels, and those who do not are not always on the side of the demons. Yet even if the toleration concepts are neither automatically commendatory nor automatically pejorative, as 21–24 show, these concepts do not seem to be completely neutral either. In the United States most people's intuitive feeling is that toleration has a commendatory, while intoleration a pejorative, bent.

It is not easy to fathom why it should seem this way. Certainly taking first one and then the other point of view (as in chap. 2) offers little help. Those who are not tolerated will certainly see toleration as a state deserving of a commendation, but those who are intolerant will hardly think the same way. As to those who are tolerated, they might or might not view their state as worthy of praise. If they are newly tolerated they might still feel grateful, but if they have experienced toleration for a long period, they may wish for a form of acceptance and thus see toleration as a halfway house full of suspicion and insecurity. Similarly, those who tolerate might or might not view their own state as a happy one. Those near the border of intoleration will see toleration as onerous, while those farther from it might feel more comfortable. Overall, therefore, the point of view approach does not seem to offer an explanation of why some of the toleration concepts might lean nonneutrally either in the commendatory or pejorative direction.

The reason-giving approach is even less promising because, give and take a little, all four forms of reason giving that support toleration run parallel with all four forms supporting intoleration. In other words, no conclusive argument seems to justify our intuitive feeling that toleration carries more commendatory meaning than intoleration. This absence of a conclusive argument suggests that the source of these feelings may be social and/or political instead. That is, it could be that toleration has achieved its commendatory status, if indeed it has, mainly because many of the leaders, the literature, the institutions, and even the people of the American society in which we live have a liberal outlook. (We will discuss the meaning of *liberal* in chap. 8.) However commendatory toleration has become, it should be clear that, nonetheless, it cannot become completely commendatory because all societies need to be intolerant of some things in order to survive. If a society tolerated all forms of killing, lying, and property taking, it would no doubt quickly disintegrate.[1] Still, if the primary source of toleration's commendatory sheen is social in the sense specified above, we can expect this meaning to vary from time to time and from place to place. We can even expect that in times of prolonged crisis, when discipline and sacrifice are needed, toleration could lose its commendatory aura to intoleration.

Whichever way it goes, the commendatory or pejorative meaning of the toleration concepts will not be a function simply of people's views about them. These concepts are tied analytically to other concepts in such a way that it is impossible for them to avoid bearing some of the aura of meaning of these other concepts. This point can be best understood by

ANALYSIS

focusing initially on 'intoleration'. To act intolerantly is to attempt to restrain others, that is, to seek to deprive them of their freedom through the use of some form of coercion. So, when one is justly called intolerant, he or she is not just stuck with one pejorative label but with others as well. Similarly, in a society in which toleration is considered commendatory (because, perhaps, people are seen as taking the trouble to rein in their negative attitudes and to do so for the benefit of others), those who are tolerant will be praised not only as tolerant people but also as champions of freedom, self-expression, and pluralism and as opponents of coercion.

But these behavioral concepts tell only part of the story. To return once more to those who are intolerant, their feelings and attitudes usually match their intolerant behavior. In part, they are intolerant behaviorally because they disapprove of those they do not tolerate. More than that, they may even have contempt for, be disgusted with, and look down upon those they do not tolerate. To the extent that these attitudes have a negative connotation, to that extent they are likely to infect intoleration with this same tarnish.

It does not follow that if intoleration is badly infected, toleration is completely free. There is a big difference between the behavioral and attitudinal sides of these concepts. Behaviorally, as we have just seen, intoleration and toleration differ greatly. Thus, if a society condemns behavioral intoleration and all of the concepts linked with it, it will most likely praise behavioral toleration. But the contemptuous attitudes and negative feelings of intolerant people are not matched by respectful attitudes and feelings on the part of tolerant people. Although the various toleration states differ with respect to the kinds of attitudes and feelings that they contain, none will completely avoid negative emotion directed toward those who are tolerated. At best, the attitudes and feelings will be neutral and at worst negative. Indeed, tolerant people may feel as much contempt for those they tolerate as intolerant

56

people feel for those who are the object of their intolerant behavior.

Overall, then, even in a so-called liberal society, the toleration concepts will be commendatory but not unreservedly so. Their main positive force will come from their association with concepts such as freedom and from whatever commendatory meaning the society places upon the state of tolerating. However, because the attitudes and feelings that we have when tolerating are not necessarily admirable, even to the liberal, the image of the concept will likely be somewhat stained. We will have more to say about these matters in chapter 8 when we deal directly with liberal ideology.

On Being Both Tolerant and Intolerant

In addition to helping explain when and why the toleration concepts are commendatory or pejorative, the analysis of reasons in this and the previous chapter is useful in another way. Before it became clear that there are different forms of toleration, it might have seemed that a person or society must fall either on one side or the other of the toleration frontier. Yet once we realize that radically different reasons can support both toleration and intoleration, it is evident that people can be both tolerant and intolerant (not-tolerant) at the same time. Undoubtedly some tolerant people are tolerant in all four reason-giving ways. But it is conceivable that others are tolerant (and even extremely so) methodologically but intolerant in matters of morals. It is also conceivable that still others are tolerant tactically and prudentially but intolerant in the realm of moral concerns. Other combinations are possible. Some may have come to believe that morally we ought to be tolerant, because individual rights in many matters should receive very high priority, but that we ought to be intolerant in business and in other practical areas.

57

So if a person (or a society) is to be labeled tolerant, some specification of the nature of the toleration practiced is in order, at least on the level of the kinds of reasons identified in this and the previous chapter. Actually, further specification is in order because someone can be both tolerant and intolerant on any given reason-giving level. This mixture of the tolerant and intolerant is most readily found on the normative level. John may be intolerant of certain things such as attacks on freedom of speech, military spending, and pollution and yet be tolerant of other things such as sexual behavior, drug use, and various religious practices. John might not wish to admit openly that he is both tolerant and intolerant. Especially if he lives in a tolerant milieu, he may wish to think of himself as tolerant. If so, he may use words other than *intolerant* to characterize certain aspects of his behavior and attitude. He may, for example, not see himself as intolerant of those who deprive others of their freedom of speech but may rather view himself as acting to protect the rights of those who would speak if they could. He may seek to wear the mantle of the tolerant person even if objectively he could be characterized as both tolerant and intolerant.

This particular condition of being on both sides of the toleration border should not be confused with another form that has nothing to do with reason giving. Actually there are two non-reason-giving forms. One exists because many of the things we tolerate (or do not tolerate) can be tolerated (or not-tolerated) in more than one way. If Sam's smoking bothers the rest of us, but we rarely speak up about the problem and at most apply only minor social pressure to get him to stop, are we tolerant or not? Because we are trying to stop him, it would seem that we are intolerant even if mildly so. Yet because we refrain from confiscating Sam's cigars and cigar money, and we certainly avoid applying physical force to keep him from smoking, we also seem tolerant. In a similar vein, if a country applies limited political and economic pressure on another country in order to get it to come into line with its policies toward terrorists but refuses to take stronger measures, including military ones, is it tolerant or intolerant? Again it is difficult to say. Perhaps the best way to speak here is that in one way it is tolerant, in another intolerant.

The second form of border fudging not related to reason giving results from psychological indecision. A person can be intolerant one day and tolerant the next. Abe speaks up on Monday about his wife's incessant chatter, but on Tuesday he simply sits back and bites on his cigar. There is nothing spectacularly original about noting these constant border crossings. It is just that, inasmuch as toleration and intoleration are border concepts, we should not be surprised, indeed we should expect, to find more than the normal number of such crossings in settings where these concepts have application.

Intoleration and Coercion

Though we have associated the concept of intoleration with coercion in this chapter, it would be a mistake to suppose that this association is one of identity. Although certain uses of *intolerant* imply the use of coercion (e.g., "He acted intolerably" does imply this, but "He has an intolerant attitude" does not), the use of coercion does not imply that someone has acted intolerantly. More than likely, little old ladies get mugged not because their assailants are intolerant of them but because the muggers want what is in their purses. In addition to coercive acts done selfishly, those done whimsically also do not fall under the aegis of intoleration.

Still, although acting intolerantly and using coercion are not the same, considerable overlap is present—for instance, when we deal intolerantly with misbehaving children (adults, groups, etc.). We can act intolerantly with children in general if we feel that, as a lot, they tend to be noisy, demanding, and terribly expensive to feed and clothe, and we then translate

59

these feelings into behavior. But what if we genuinely love our children and yet are forced to use coercion in order to keep them from hurting themselves? Is this intolerant behavior? Are we intolerant when we lovingly enforce rules to keep them from playing with matches, running by themselves across busy streets, playing with older children who are engaged in petty crime?

The following point suggests not. Although coercion is being used here to keep our little ones from hurting themselves, and although we disapprove of what they are doing, because our disapproval does not carry with it a sense of disgust, disparagement, or lack of respect for them, it seems wrong to label our response intolerant. Instead we tend to look for other, softer, labels to characterize what we are doing—such as *not allowing* and *not permitting*. If, again, our love gives way to negative emotions because of the demands they make upon our time, energies, and financial condition, then we tend to slide into using not only *intolerant* but also other expressions that we associate with that concept such as *can't put up with, can't stand,* and *can't abide.*

Yet, it must be admitted that our tendencies are not all in one direction. Especially if we focus our attention exclusively upon the child's unacceptable behavior, we might very well say, "We are intolerant of that kind of behavior." Usage appears fuzzy in these contexts. Much the same can be said about our dealings with those whom we treat paternalistically.[2] When we coerce those adults we care much for, so that they will not harm themselves, we are reluctant to, although we still might, label our actions intolerant. However, when we paternalistically coerce those we look down upon (e.g., drunks, hooligans) our reluctance diminishes. The paradigm uses of 'intolerant', 'intolerance', and 'intolerable' do seem, therefore, to require that both coercion and a sense of disgust with those exhibiting unacceptable behavior be present.

Overview 5

Summary

The various toleration concepts are highly complex. Because of this complexity we believe it is helpful to summarize and structure the discussions of chapters 1–4. The summary will concentrate upon key distinctions that help to generate the various toleration concepts, while the structuring will take the form of definition-like characterizations of key toleration concepts.

The most basic distinctions either separate those cases where some toleration concept can be applied from those where none can or they separate the positive and negative sides of the concepts of toleration. Put roughly, the toleration concepts do not have an application when a person (or group) is not in position to react to something either behaviorally or attitudinally. Partly because of this feature, and partly because these concepts focus our attention on the agent or actor more than the situation being judged (as do some other evaluative concepts), they have a responsive or reactive character.

Yet even if a person can react, these concepts do not have application if that person is not affected by something or, if affected, is indifferent to it. In the latter case we are more likely to speak of condoning rather than tolerating the behavior in question. When the toleration concepts have application, their positive side has the feature of grudging "acceptance." Tolerating implies less than full acceptance of some person, object, action, policy, characteristic, or whatever. Although some of its forms appear less grudging than others,

61

and in fact may accommodate neutral acceptance, there is a limit to the amount of acceptance that the toleration concepts will tolerate. When, for example, we wholeheartedly accept the religious views of others, we join them and, in this sense, transcend toleration. To accept something fully is, as we have characterized it, to escape toleration out the back door.

We escape toleration out the front door when we do not tolerate others. However, the negative side of the concept of toleration can, again speaking roughly, be divided into three parts. One part is characterized by such words as *coercion* and *constraint*. In this case, those exhibiting unacceptable behavior are coerced in one way or another, and those engaged in coercion are said to be acting intolerantly. The second is characterized by such words as *retreat, retirement,* and *withdrawal*. With this form, when we cannot stand, put up with, or tolerate something, we disengage ourselves from it. The third part is characterized by such words as *negotiation* and *positive reinforcement*. Here those exhibiting untoward behavior are offered a reward if they will cease and desist.

This same division of retreat, coercion, and positive reinforcement is not mirrored on the toleration side. This difference occurs because when we tolerate, we must not coerce others, not withdraw, *and* not make deals to stop undesirable behavior. That is, we cannot be said to be tolerant just because we have not, for example, coerced others. The mirroring also fails to hold because, on the negative side, as we increasingly reject a point of view or type of behavior, we become increasingly intolerant. On the other side, in contrast, increasing nonrejection yields increasing toleration only up to a point and then moves into acceptance. There is no back door out of not-tolerating.

The application of the toleration concepts is not limited to situations where we can respond behaviorally in one way or another. Their scope extends to situations where we can (in terms of behavior) do little but can at least control our attitudes. In this sense, we can speak of a person having or not having a tolerant attitude toward his or her imprisonment. The toleration concepts also apply to people's character. Tolerant people may, for one reason or another, not always act in a tolerating fashion. Yet they are disposed, other things being equal, to exhibit tolerating behavior, just as people who are not tolerant usually, but not always, are disposed to exhibit not-tolerating behavior.

Yet, at least on the positive side, the meaning of these concepts as applied to personal character is not exhausted merely by saying that they are concerned with how people are disposed to behave. Tolerating people, especially those we might call very tolerant, need not have negative attitudes toward those things, creatures, people, groups they tolerate. At times, the looseness of these concepts seems to allow these people to be called tolerant even when their attitudes toward what they tolerate are neutral or indifferent. It may also be that looseness in the application of this concept is present because tolerant people's behavior is easily confused with the behavior of those we call easygoing. Whatever the explanation, the character sense, and to a lesser extent the attitudinal sense, of the concept of toleration seems to carry a broader meaning than does the behavioral sense.

The toleration concepts are complex because they contain these various senses and because the positive and the negative sides do not mirror one another in all respects. Furthermore, their complexity increases when the matter of reason giving is considered. Strictly speaking, the kinds of reasons given for and against tolerating need not be part of the meaning of these concepts. Yet the four kinds of reasons for tolerating are sufficiently different from each other that they seem to generate four different kinds of toleration. People tolerate in order to:

1. gain further information (methodological-procedural toleration);
2. manipulate others or themselves (tactical-empirical toleration);
3. satisfy personal preferences (personal-prudential toleration); and/or
4. exercise moral and other value options (normative toleration).

These four forms of tolerating are mirrored fairly closely on the negative or not-tolerating side.

In addition to analyzing the toleration concepts in terms of types of responses (chap.1) and reasons given for responding one way or another (chaps. 3 and 4), we found it useful to analyze these concepts from the perspective of the participants themselves (chap. 2). Although we granted that each participant could view his/her role from more than one perspective, several unique viewpoints were identified. From the point of view of those who are tolerating, for instance, their lives are filled with struggle. They may find themselves pressured to continue tolerating, to tolerate even more, or even to transcend their tolerating completely. Given these kinds of pressures we might expect tolerators of this sort to warn those they tolerate not to push them to the limit. Warnings are also likely to be issued by those who do not tolerate others, only this time issued to their friends, about the evils of tolerating. Those who are intolerant are also likely to condemn toleration as well as those who would urge them to transform themselves into tolerators. As to those who are not tolerated, they may see toleration as a good state, but once they join the ranks of the tolerated, their views can, and likely will, change considerably. Thus toleration can be viewed as better than nothing, but not a whole lot better.

A family portrait of the toleration concepts (fig. 1) exhibits many of the preceding points but especially the basic one

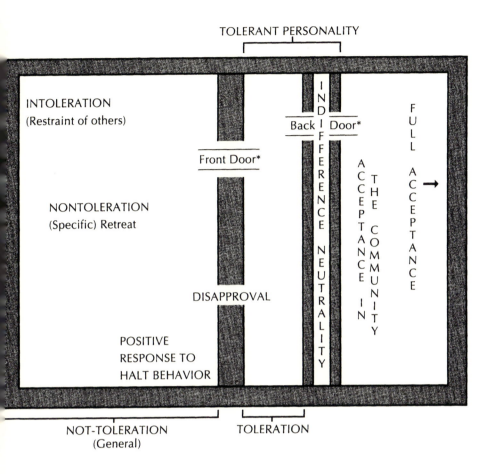

FIGURE 1. Family Relations of Toleration Concepts

*It should be understood that the two-doors analogy is misleading in one sense, because some people move from the left side of the diagram to the right side and vice versa without visiting the middle.

about the tripartite nature of these concepts (i.e., not-toleration—toleration—acceptance).

Formal Characterizations

A more formal way of characterizing some of the toleration concepts follows. We offer these characterizations to reemphasize the complexity and variety of these concepts. We also offer them as a reference. As such, this quick overview will suffice to give our readers a sense of what is to be learned from these characterizations.

X is *acting* (acted) *intolerantly* toward Y where (it is presupposed that):

1. X and Y are individuals and/or groups;
2. X and Y are not identical; *and*
3. X is mature enough to make judgments (rational or otherwise) while Y is some living organism (speaking narrowly) or almost any object (speaking broadly); and

when:

1. Y acts (or fails to act) or moves (or fails to move)
2. so that others (especially X) and/or Y are affected (mentioning Y makes paternalistic responses possible)
3. in such a way (in ways) that X disapproves of Y's behavior mentioned in 1
4. with an attitude of disdain, disgust, contempt, or outrage (this condition is usually but not always present)
5. and X attempts (coercively) to intervene directly or indirectly (i.e., through others) to alter the behavior in 1 (where the act of intervention is physical or verbal)
6. for any one or more of the four basic reasons (i.e.,

66

procedural, tactical, prudential, and normative) or for no reason at all (in the sense that X may not be able to give reasons).

The comparable analyses of someone (or some group) "being intolerant" (in the dispositional sense) and "being extremely intolerant" differ in several respects.

X is intolerant (or X is an intolerant person or organization) where (it is presupposed that):

see the "where" conditions of acting intolerantly above; and

when:

1. a variety of people (Ys) are acting or failing to act (and secondarily a variety of creatures or objects are moving or failing to move)
2. so that others (especially X) and/or Y are affected
3. in such a way (in ways) that X disapproves of many of the forms of behavior mentioned in 1
4. with an attitude of disdain, disgust, contempt, or outrage (this condition is more likely to be satisfied than with intolerant action)
5. and X attempts (coercively) to intervene directly and/or indirectly (i.e., through others) to alter many of the forms of behavior mentioned in 1 (where these acts of intervention are physical and/or verbal)
6. for any one or more of the four basic reasons (i.e., procedural, tactical, prudential, and normative) or for no reason at all (in the sense that X may not be able to give reasons).

"X is *extremely intolerant*" (given the "where" presuppositions and the "when" conditions above) means the same as "acted intolerantly" except that:

1. the items under condition 1 above are very numerous (X is intolerant, as we might be tempted to say, about everything and everybody);
2. X is intolerant (to a higher degree than most) about self-regarding matters;
3. X's negative attitudes (condition 4) are extreme; and/or
4. X's interventionist practices (condition 5) are extreme (X tends, for example, to imprison and torture people rather than merely verbally reprimanding them).

Presumably various combinations are possible here. It would be rare indeed if an extremely intolerant person became so because his/her behavior fell only under one of the above exceptions.

The analysis of the general sense of "could not tolerate" is similar to acting intolerantly with one exception.

X could *not tolerate* Y (any longer) where (it is presupposed that):

same as the "where" conditions above for "acting intolerantly" and the "when" condition 5 of "acting intolerantly" is modified to read:

5a. X intervenes (i.e., acts intolerantly), withdraws, *or* offers a positive reward for getting the behavior in 1 to stop.

There is a more specific sense of "not tolerate" that is identical with the general sense except that condition 5 of "acting intolerantly" is now modified to read:

5b. X withdraws or offers a positive reward for getting the behavior in 1 to stop.

The characterization of "was (is) tolerant" shows that several of the conditions differ significantly from "acting intolerantly."

X was (is) tolerant of Y where (it is presupposed that):

1. X and Y are individuals and/or groups;
2. X and Y are not identical; *and*
3. X is mature enough to make judgments (rational or otherwise) while Y is some living organism (speaking narrowly) or almost any object (speaking broadly); and

when:

1. Y acts or fails to act (or moves or fails to move)
2. so that others (usually and/or especially X) and/or Y are affected (paternalism is excluded here because condition 5 below no longer includes coercion, even though Y may be the one or one of the ones affected)
3. with an attitude of disdain, disgust, contempt, or outrage (this condition is even less necessary than for acting intolerantly),
4. and X does little or nothing to intervene, does not withdraw, and does not make Y any positively reinforcing deals
5. for any one or more of the four basic reasons identified (procedural, tactical, prudential, and normative) or for no reason at all (in the sense that X may not be able to give reasons).

The analysis of someone (or some group) "being tolerant" (in the dispositional sense) differs only slightly from (acting) in a tolerant fashion.

"X is tolerant" (or "X is a tolerant person or group"), given the "where" presuppositions and the "when" conditions above, means the same as "is tolerant" except that:

1. X's disapproval of the behavior of various Ys in condition 3 is probably diminished;
2. the special attitude toward various Ys (condition 4) is also probably diminished and may not even be present; and
3. X intervenes, withdraws, and makes deals (condition 5) only rarely if at all.

To be extremely tolerant is an extension of being tolerant in the dispositional sense of that concept.

"X is extremely tolerant" (or "X is an extremely tolerant person or group"), given the "where" presuppositions and the "when" conditions, means the same as "is tolerant" except that:

1. the items under condition 1 are very numerous (that X is tolerant, we are tempted to say, about everything and everybody);
2. X's disapproval under condition 3 is still more muted than for being tolerant dispositionally and may in fact be neutral; and
3. X rarely, if ever, takes an action (by intervening, retreating, or dealing) with respect to the wide variety of items under condition 1.

The third major concept with which we have been dealing is acceptance.

X has accepted what Y has done where (it is presupposed that):

1. X and Y are individuals and/or groups;
2. X and Y are not identical; and
3. X is mature enough to make judgments (rational or

otherwise) while Y is some living organism (speaking narrowly) or almost any object (speaking broadly); and

when:

1. Y acts (or fails to act) or moves (or fails to move)
2. so that others (usually and/or especially X) and/or Y are affected (paternalism is excluded here because condition 5 below no longer includes coercion even though Y may be the one or one of the ones affected)
3. in such a way (in ways) that X approves of Y's behavior mentioned in 1
4. with a positive attitude of respect, admiration, and the like for Y (though it is not absolutely clear that this condition is necessary);
5. X takes steps to support Y's activities mentioned in 1
6. for any one or more of the four basic reasons identified (procedural, tactical, prudential, and normative) or for no reason at all (in the sense that X may not be able to give reasons).

"X is an accepting person," given the "where" presuppositions and the "when" conditions, means the same as "has accepted" except that:

1. the items under 1 above are numerous (or very numerous depending on how extremely accepting X is); and
2. X supports many of the behavior forms mentioned in 1 in many different ways.

Part II

ISSUES & ARGUMENTS

Historical Perspective

6

Religious, Political, and Social Toleration

Our principal goal in the previous chapters was to gain an understanding of what the toleration concepts are, how they are related to one another, and the way they function in our thinking. Because the mode of analysis was primarily personal discourse, our focus was on the role of tolerating in the day-to-day lives of individuals. This perspective was both necessary and useful for untangling the features of toleration and its family of related concepts.

However, these concepts can also play a role in moral and political debate when they move from the clutter of ordinary life to the anxious focus of public controversy. Their public role is neither as common nor as universal as their place in ordinary life. This role has arisen in the culture and politics of Western European history as the result of a lengthy and complex development. This historical development established the role of tolerating in Europe and fixed the patterns of argument in which debates about tolerating are undertaken. This process is, therefore, central to an understanding of the particular nature of tolerating in Western Europe. Its importance mandates that, in the remainder of this chapter, we take a brief look at its history and the patterns of argument that it has established. Subsequent chapters will continue to look at the public role of toleration.

In Western European history, the public issue of toleration was addressed in three major areas: religion, politics, and social relations. In historical terms the debate concerning religious toleration came first. The issue of religious toleration (and intolerance) became important with the rise of Christianity and, in part, became an issue precisely because of the special features of the new religion. Christianity differed from previous religions in purporting to be the religion of all human beings rather than of a particular tribe, state, or people.[1] In the ancient world, no clear distinction occurred between citizenship, religious belief, and cultural heritage. To be a citizen of Athens one had to be born a citizen of that city, participate in its religious ceremonies, and enjoy its culture. In fact, the tie between citizenship and religion was so strong that people were barred from participating in government if they failed to take part in the series of religious rituals that took place in the spring of each year.[2]

By claiming to be universal, however, the Christian church made possible a distinction between religious affiliation and the ties of citizenship and therefore opened the way for conflicts between the demands of the two loyalties. If the universal scope of the Christian church made tolerating conceptually possible, its relations with the Roman Empire made the issue historically alive. While the Romans were more cosmopolitan than the Greeks in being unconcerned with the proliferation of sects and cults within the empire, they nonetheless required that all pay obeisance to the state gods as a sign of loyalty and good citizenship. This the Christians refused to do, and their refusal in part led to the persecution they suffered until the time of Constantine.[3]

The universality of the Christian church paved the way for a second feature of Christianity that had a major impact on the issue of religious toleration. This is the distinction between spiritual and secular authority, as encapsulated in Christ's teaching, "Render unto Caesar that which is Caesar's, and render unto God that which is God's."[4] Much subsequent conflict concerning toleration resulted from either insisting on this separation of secular and sacred authority—entailing a policy of toleration on the part of the secular powers—or denying this distinction and insisting on a necessary unity of the authority of the Church and the Prince. Obviously, neither differing branches of the Christian church nor differing religious leaders (e.g., Luther) kept consistently to one side of this argument or the other.[5]

So in a sense, both the universality of the Christian church and its sometime insistence on the separation of sacred and secular authority lent support to a policy of toleration of religion. However, the new religion contained a third feature that undermined toleration and in some ways made it less tolerant than the old pagan religions. This feature was its insistence on doctrinal uniformity and purity. In contrast, most of the pagan and polytheistic religions were less concerned with correctness or uniformity of belief than with correctness of ritual practice or the preservation of religious institutions.[6]

The history of the impassioned struggles regarding toleration within the Christian church is too long and intricate to be examined fully here. The rise of Protestantism in Europe, with its emphasis on the centrality of the individual conscience in religious belief, contributed eventually to the culmination of the struggle concerning religious toleration and a shift to political toleration as the new arena of discussion. Also contributing to bringing about toleration was the realization, partly within but largely outside the church, that the religious wars of the time were too costly and bloody.

In any case, the culmination and shift took place in the seventeenth century, though in many ways the issue of political toleration arose from and was a continuation of the earlier debate.[7] Arguments concerning religious toleration did not end at this time, of course, and important religious conflicts remain. What happened is simply that the focus and emphasis of the debate shifted in a significant way. This shift can be marked by two events, one political and one intellectual, that occurred in Great Britain near the end of the century. The

77

political event is the passage of the Bill of "Indulgence to Dissenters" by Parliament in 1689 that settled, in the English-speaking world at least, the issue of religious toleration.[8]

The intellectual event was the publication of John Locke's *A Letter Concerning Toleration* also in 1689.[9] Many of the major features of the political philosophy of liberalism were developed in the debates that focused on the issue of religious toleration. These issues were nicely comingled in the person of Locke, who was an advocate of both religious and political toleration. Indeed, the impact of Locke's work lay not in any novelty of its arguments or perspectives but in his development of these arguments in a systematic and thorough fashion. The key to Locke's stance in both areas was his emphasis on the self-directing and independent individual who ought to be free from coercion by the state in all save a few well-defined areas.[10]

As a result of these two events, the issues of tolerating were no longer confined to matters of religion but encompassed secular political concerns as well. Whereas the earlier Christian claim of a universal religious doctrine had opened a gap between the individual and the social order in the matter of religion, the later liberal claim of the universal capacity of reason opened up another gap between the individual and the social order in the matter of political allegiance. Now the central issue was not the individual's relationship to the church but of his or her relationship to the state. Correspondingly, in matters of toleration, a shift occured away from appealing to conscience and toward a process of democratic decision making.

Beginning in the nineteenth century and continuing to the twentieth, the scope of the debate on toleration shifted once more. Here the seminal figure was John Stuart Mill and the seminal work was *On Liberty*. Mill was not concerned with religious or political repression; he did not consider these the major problems of his day. He was concerned rather with the various forms of subtle oppression that society as a whole exerts on the life of the individual. He complained that "Our merely social intolerance kills no one, roots out no opinions, but induces men to disguise them, or to abstain from any active effort in their diffusion. . . . But the price paid for this sort of intellectual pacification is the sacrifice of the entire moral courage of the human mind."[11]

But Mill was concerned with more than freedom of expression. In addition, he was concerned with the attempt to open up freedom for varying ways of living, including the freedom to adopt differing moral codes. He claimed: "As it is useful that while mankind are imperfect there should be different opinions, so it is that there should be different experiments in living . . . ; and that the worth of different modes of life should be proved practically, when anyone thinks to try them."[12] Mill was so taken with this idea that he was moved to a celebration of eccentricity, proclaiming: "Eccentricity has always abounded when and where strength of character has abounded; and the amount of eccentricity in a society has generally been proportional to the amount of genius, mental vigor and moral courage which it contained."[13]

Mill was concerned with universal development of individual character, the relationship between individual freedom and social authority, and finally with the positive celebration of variety itself, even to include eccentricity. In these ways, his views echoed themes of earlier debates, just as, since World War II, Mill's views are heard echoing in the United States in the fascination many people have with alternative modes of life or experiments in living but also with two specific issues of moral toleration. The first is whether immoral practices can be tolerated by communities. This is the issue that has been addressed in Great Britain in the famous Hart/Devlin debates.[14] The second is the issue of civil disobedience that spawned a huge body of literature in the United

States in the latter portion of the 1960s and in the early portion of the 1970s.[15]

Thus, the debate on toleration moved over the centuries from religion to politics to society. But it developed in a second way as well. The early religious arguments focused on the question of whether obnoxious, erroneous, or injurious beliefs should be tolerated. This question gave way to the liberal issue of whether these beliefs could be voiced on street corners, in print, or among groups of individuals who held them in common. In the political context, therefore, the issue was not merely one of belief but of speech.

Yet even the classical liberals thought they knew where to draw the line of the limits of toleration. Voicing and propagating noxious opinions must be tolerated, they thought, but acting on these beliefs is another matter and need not be tolerated at all.[16] But this view leads to difficulties: if we believe that an individual ought to be allowed to hold on to his or her own views, voice, and even propagate them, on what grounds can we justify preventing him or her from acting on them? Indeed, the focus of the debate on toleration has become that of our obligation to tolerate individuals who act on beliefs that we believe to be erroneous, immoral, or wrongheaded. That is, the arena of toleration has changed from belief to speech to action.

Spheres of Responsibility

Although in the course of history the debate was concerned with many different kinds of toleration, the arguments that actually were marshaled by all sides fall roughly into three categories: the issues of spheres of responsibility, the questions of freedom of conscience, and what we have termed "pragmatic" issues of whether toleration leads to good or to harmful results. We will give brief consideration to each of these categories in turn.

Many of the issues concerning what is and is not to be tolerated turn on questions of who has what set of responsibilities and of the range of these sets of responsibility. An instructor may, for example, claim in desperation that she cannot tolerate loud talking in her classroom because it is her responsibility to maintain good order there. Yet this same person may note sadly that she has no choice but to tolerate the brutal methods that her neighbor uses to discipline his children because the affairs of this family are not her responsibility. The responsibilities that we possess may be legal, moral, social, religious, or personal. They may change and fluctuate with time and circumstance. On some occasions we may be in doubt concerning what we ought or ought not to tolerate simply because we are uncertain about the exact range of our responsibilities. If an employee of a large auto manufacturer has reason to believe that it uses unsafe gasoline tanks, does he or she have any responsibility to do anything about it, and, if so, what kind of responsibility?

Obviously, arguments about spheres of responsibility will have application more for our actions than our attitudes because they concern what we are obligated to do. More specifically, their thrust will be to portray the classical responses to questions about the nature and extent of the responsibility (1) the individual has to others, to various institutions in society, and to the state itself and (2) institutions and the state have to individuals, other institutions, and other states. There are two extreme responses to these questions. The first is radical individualism. With this response a great deal of tolerating of the individual is required. The second is collectivism. With it, little or no tolerating of the individual by the society is required. Several intermediate positions reside between these two extremes, though only one will be mentioned here: pluralism.

As best exemplified in the writings of Robert Nozick in recent times, two fundamental and related ideas appear to pro-

81

vide the basis of the radical individualists' view.[17] The first is that no one may interfere with the individual in performance of actions that concern only him or her. Nozick and others in this tradition often use spatial metaphors, such as the image of a private space or bubble that encloses each individual and within which he or she may perform whatever acts are desired without interference from others.[18] It is usually assumed by those who espouse this view that the bubble of personal privacy is significantly large—although it is not always clear just how large it is. The second, allied notion of the radical individualists is that we are justified in entering the personal space of others, and others are justified in entering our own space, only by means of the mutual and freely granted consent of those directly involved in the transaction.[19]

The implications of this view for a theory of tolerating are clear. It would appear to require a good deal of tolerating of the individual by other individuals and by societies. Whatever their beliefs, likes, dislikes, fears, interests, and so forth, others will be required to tolerate whatever occurs within our bubble of private space and whatever mutually agreed-upon activities we should undertake with others. The limits of that which need not be tolerated are also pretty distinct. We need not tolerate those actions that affect either ourselves or others without consent.[20]

Although it is not entirely clear how large the bubble of personal space is supposed to be, it is apparent that those who accept the radical individualist point of view mean to include the three main historical topics of the debate on toleration (religion, politics, and morality) within the range of the private sphere.[21] Religious views and activity, political views and activity, and moral beliefs and activity are all included within the domain of that which is essentially to be tolerated. The plausibility of the individualist's inclusion of these activities within the sphere of the private depends in part on an interpretation of these activities as essentially private. Religion, for example, is understood as an essentially personal affair having to do with the relationship the individual has to the divinity. Political matters also are concerned with personal views and personally sanctioned associations. Morality, furthermore, is conceived of as something that is essentially private. It is a matter, mainly, of leaving others alone and tending to one's own business. In this sort of morality the ideas of respect, fairness, and the like are highly regarded, but the concepts of kindness, benevolence, or duty to others are not.[22]

The radical individualists have provided a variety of answers to the question of why the individual's personal space should be respected, but not all of the answers are compatible with one another. Perhaps the most widely known answer, provided by Mill, depends for its plausibility on a moral principle and an empirical prediction. Mill's moral principle, of course, is that we are obliged to act to produce the greatest good for the greatest number.[23] His empirical prediction is that if others attempt to interfere with those actions that are self-regarding, they will inevitably fail to produce good and will cause harm instead.[24]

The second extreme perspective is the collectivist. It encompasses a group of three closely related ideas, the first being that a society or a culture is an organic whole of interdependent segments.[25] On this view it is impossible to separate the duties of citizenship from the rites of religion, for example, or from the enjoyment of cultural activity. Contemporary Islamic theocracies, as in Iran or Saudi Arabia, make no distinction between religion and citizenship.[26] Or, the legal system of the Soviet Union was considered part of the state's apparatus for shaping the character of citizens and was therefore legitimately under the ultimate control of the Communist party.[27]

The second basic collectivist idea is that what is valuable

and distinctive in human culture is the product of the society as a whole—rather than being the contributions of particular individuals or groups of individuals.[28] Consider, as an example, the Marxist view that human ideologies, human arts, and human ways of life are fundamentally the product of the economic relations within societies.[29] Or consider the Roman Catholic view that proper religious activity cannot be undertaken by the isolated individual but only by means of the encompassing activity of the church as a whole.[30] Hegel's view, of course, is that the development of history occurs via the movement of the Absolute, which, though it may utilize the talents of one individual or another, operates through the medium of the entire human race.[31]

The final collectivist idea is that each human individual is the product of, and dependent upon, society. The particular person is not, as in the individualist view, self-contained and self-created but is rather the product of social forces and the cultural environment in which he or she is nurtured.[32]

As might be expected, the collectivist's views concerning what is to be tolerated are quite nearly the mirror opposite of the individualist's. The collectivist would see little reason to tolerate the beliefs or actions of particular individuals. These are of little consequence whether from a religious, moral, or political perspective. What does require tolerating are the activities and ideologies of societies, and this tolerating is required both of individuals and of other social entities. The activities and integrity of the society, on this view, must remain free from interference, while those actions or beliefs that threaten or thwart society cannot be tolerated. The particular attitudes and activities of the human individual, on this view, need not be tolerated.[33]

It goes almost without saying that the major topics of tolerating in Western Europe—religion, politics, and morality— are, for the collectivist, squarely in the realm of the social.

From the collectivist viewpoint, any realm of private activity that might exist would be so trivial as to be unworthy of toleration, particularly if it should happen to conflict with any of the concerns of the public realm. As illustrated by conditions in the present-day collectivist society of China, the realm of the private is relatively small, as it was in the Soviet Union before its recent political upheaval. In these societies there was no theoretical limit to that which may be considered of public interest and therefore part of the public domain.[34]

A third perspective on spheres of responsibility makes use of a different spatial metaphor. We can also imagine society as composed of a number of intermediate-sized bubbles containing a number of individuals (though less than the entire society) and each addressing concerns wider than those of the particular individual (though, once more, not so many as to include all of society). This view is, of course, pluralism. It was formulated by British and American political theorists in the last century and was seen specifically as an intermediate position.[35] Several ideas are central to the pluralist view.

First, the pluralists are sensitive to the collectivist argument that human individuals are not the totally self-sufficient, autonomous beings envisaged in the individualist position. Pluralists believe that individuals have little power by themselves and that their lives and destinies are powerfully shaped by the societies around them.[36]

Yet, second, the pluralists differ from the collectivists in that they do not view society as one monolithic whole but rather as a collection of smaller wholes or groups such as religious organizations, ethnic groups, educational institutions, labor unions, business organizations, and so forth. Society, in this view, is an aggregate of these lesser wholes.[37] These groups hold the real power in society and are able to give shape and direction to individual lives. Thus, although individuals may be members of one or several of these groups,

85

they can gain influence and significance within society only by participating in them.

Third, pluralists insist that society is an arena of competition within which the various social groups strive to advance their group interests.[38] In the collectivist view relatively little significant competition occurs within a society: there cannot be competition if society is a monolithic entity. In the individualist view, in contrast, competition exists, but it is between individuals rather than among groups.

The manner in which pluralism is meliorist is thus clear. It emphasizes the lack of power and the dependent nature of particular human beings, yet it does not thereby place them at the mercy of a monolithic society. Rather it puts them under the protection and nurture of smaller, more specialized groups within society. Still, even though persons are not independent and self-directing as the individualists thought, particular social groups, because of their limited scope and multiplicity, cannot expect to have the control over the particular individual that might be sought in a collectivist society.[39]

The kinds of tolerating and not-tolerating justified in the pluralist position can be clearly spelled out. Individuals within groups do not necessarily have a claim on being tolerated, for the social groups may see fit to allow little individual dissent or deviancy. What is important is that the social groups themselves can claim the right to be tolerated as they pursue their various goals. Furthermore, because this view acknowledges no organic social whole, the society as a whole has no claim to be tolerated.[40]

The major argument that the pluralists present to support their position is that it provides the best and most realistic model in terms of which individuals within society and segments of society can effectively protect their interests and advance their goals. Individuals who by themselves are weak can become strong by banding together with others of similar interests to press a common cause. Also, segments of society can press their cause against others or band together with them in continually shifting alliances to seek advantage in particular cases.[41]

Freedom of Conscience

The second group of important arguments in the history of the debates over toleration concerns appeals to conscience. In particular, the issue of appealing to conscience has been central to many disputes about religious belief and practice but also, much more recently, to disputes about civil disobedience. Before considering these arguments, however, we will take note of the precise nature of an appeal to conscience.

We often appeal to conscience either to explain or justify our beliefs and actions whether to ourselves or to others. When we say, "My conscience requires that . . . ," "My conscience would not permit me to . . . ," "My conscience would bother me if . . . ," we are making appeals of a particular sort. First, we are claiming that something is either required or prohibited by a standard of belief or conduct we possess. This standard need not be a formally stated principle or even a consciously articulated one. It may simply be a feeling that something is required or prohibited. However, it is important to note that by appealing to conscience we are signaling our strong reluctance to give up this standard, no matter how ill-conceived it may appear to others. Second, the appeal to conscience is an appeal to a judgment of a certain sort, the judgment that a belief or act is required or prohibited by one's standards.

Third, in making an appeal to conscience, we are not necessarily, although often we are, making claims that these

87

standards are correct. It is the minimal claim that the standards employed are our own and that our judgments about the appropriateness of beliefs or conduct in light of these standards are correct. In appealing to conscience, we are not particularly trying to win over others to these standards. If we were, the appeal would be not to conscience but to the reasons that led us to hold to those standards.

In addition, when we say that we must act in accordance with our conscience, or we recommend to others that they follow the dictates of their consciences, we are making a formal appeal, formal in the sense that we are not recommending or denigrating any acts or beliefs in particular. In this respect, following our conscience resembles acting in accordance with Kant's Categorical Imperative. It does not directly tell us what to do or to believe but is a means of helping to determine what we should do or believe.

Finally, what makes a public appeal to conscience so important for the study of tolerating is that it is often an appeal of last resort, to be relied upon when all other approaches have failed. From our point of view, it would be far better to have won over those with whom we are at odds in some other way. It would be better for us not to have to rely on appeals to conscience but instead to convince others by offering formidable arguments. Those who are being requested to tolerate have a similar difficulty. They would be less uncomfortable and less perplexed about the correctness of what they are considering if the appeal were to reasons or arguments rather than only to someone else's conscience.

The existence of this discomfort for those who make appeals to conscience and those who are asked to tolerate does not imply that from a moral point of view acting from conscience is somehow suspect or less than worthy. Rather, when we are requesting that our beliefs or acts be tolerated by others, we often make the appeal to conscience only as a last resort. From our own perspective the appeal to conscience will not necessarily be an appeal of last resort. It will often be our first resort, for often the first question we ask ourselves when contemplating a belief or action is whether it accords with our conscience.

In the course of Western European history, those who believe that the demands of one's conscience should be tolerated by others have developed a variety of arguments. Roughly speaking these arguments fall into two main groups. The first purports to show that there are good grounds for respecting the demands of conscience. A second group purports to show that interfering with the demands of conscience is harmful.

The good-grounds arguments proceed in a number of ways. Among these are arguments of a Kantian sort. If one places a high degree of value on the use of reason by individuals, and wishes to emphasize the autonomy or freedom of individuals, it follows that one must respect the beliefs, decisions, or actions resulting from the free operation of the human intellect. To claim to value the free operation of human reason but denigrate the results of that activity is to trade in inconsistency. Therefore, many have argued that insofar as the free operation of the human intellect is valued, the results of that activity should be tolerated.[42] Notice that in this case it is not necessary to claim that the resulting beliefs, decisions, or acts are valuable, true, or worthy of respect. The claim is not that the free intellect always functions admirably or accurately but that its functioning is itself a good.

A related, also Kantian, argument is that appeals to one's conscience must, for the morally autonomous individual, be the most fundamental of all sanctions of conduct—more basic than appeals to church, state, or society. Each individual is burdened with the responsibility of determining his or her own standards of right or wrong and then acting in accordance with them. This responsibility cannot justifiably be transferred to anyone or to anything else.[43] If the authority of each individual's conscience is fundamental, then he or she cannot be expected to acquiesce in instances when others attempt to impose different standards or conclusions.

A distinct argument that has been widely used in religious as well as moral debates on tolerating proceeds as follows. A person who acts in accordance with moral or religious precepts that are believed correct (even mistakenly so), and therefore is acting in accordance with conscience, cannot be said to have acted either in a morally wrong or in a sinful manner.[44] The foundation for this view lies on a distinction between the bare physical description of an action and the state of mind of the individual who performs it. The bare physical act of killing can only properly be called murder if it is accompanied by the agent's awareness of the nature of the act and an intention to kill. A killing performed accidentally or in ignorance is simply misdescribed in usual circumstances if it is labeled murder. This much is clear and uncontroversial.

What is necessary to get this argument going is an extension of these ideas, because what persons believe to be correct is often relative to their own social standards. In our own society, a child who intentionally kills a healthy parent has unambiguously committed murder. But in certain South Pacific cultures, where the children have a duty to kill parents of a certain age, we would be misdescribing such acts if we called them murder. Even though we may justly term such acts morally wrong (in the sense that they are contrary to our own standards of morality), we cannot, according to this way of thinking, coherently describe them as immoral, because the necessary conditions for committing an immoral act are not present. Similarly, it would be very difficult to describe religious beliefs and practices that are sincerely and straightforwardly espoused by others as sinful, even though we may believe them to be foolish, mistaken, or wrongheaded.[45] It would seem then that we cannot justly punish or otherwise harm those who act in accordance with moral or religious views different from our own.

The next group of arguments about conscience purports to show that outside interference with an individual's conscience will always be harmful; this group of arguments feeds upon the earlier group by addressing an important weakness. This weakness is the failure of the group of Kantian arguments to show why individuals ought to refrain from interfering with others' acts of conscience. That is, even if the arguments are successful in demonstrating that acts and opinions of conscience ought to be respected or valued, they nonetheless do not give adequate grounds for showing why we should always refrain from interfering with them. We might plausibly argue that even that which is generally esteemed can justifiably be overridden on occasion.

Among this second group of arguments is the claim that violating a person's conscience by forcing him or her to act in ways that are contrary to his or her beliefs is *prima facie* wrong, because doing so always harms the individual involved.[46] It will harm either by causing feelings of guilt or shame as the result of acting contrary to conscience or by violating the individual's integrity. The argument is usually developed as follows. We all have beliefs about what is right or wrong, and we feel obligated to act in accordance with these beliefs. If, however, we are forced to perform acts that are morally wrong—in our own view—we will come to have feelings of shame or guilt. Notice, once more, that the force of this argument does not depend on assuming that our beliefs are necessarily true but only that we sincerely hold them and believe that they are true. Furthermore, the argument depends for its force on the view that the fact of being coerced does not diminish our feelings of guilt at having done that which is proscribed by our beliefs.

Pragmatic Arguments

Most arguments in the history of the debates on toleration probably have taken place on a less lofty and more self-interested level than those discussed previously. These arguments have not focused on the moral issues of responsibility or conscience but on the question of whether tolerating is useful—or at least not harmful—to the parties in question. Curiously, the debates focusing on pragmatic issues have not been primarily concerned with individuals but with groups of human beings, whether these be societies or institutions within societies.

In the history of the discussion on tolerating, three types of pragmatic issues have been raised. The first is whether toleration encourages the conditions that bring about the stability or survival of a society or institution. The second, closely related to the first, is concerned with how toleration affects relationships within and between groups or institutions, while the third is concerned with how policies of toleration affect the pursuit of particular values or goals within a society.

Threats to the survival of a society may be either internal or external. In the area of religion, in particular, opinion of the relative danger of various sorts of external threats has changed. The Christian church of the Middle Ages sometimes considered pagans to be a major threat to its viability, but at other times it did not. Most often, the church was more concerned with the internal threat offered by heretics. However, views of the nature of internal threats also varied considerably from time to time and from place to place.[47]

Sometimes the major internal threat was seen as that directed against the *authority* of the body in question, whether it be religious, political, or moral. Thus, in arguments concerning religious toleration of heretics, it was often claimed that heresy could not be tolerated because dissenters challenged the authority of the established religious body.[48] In failing to accept the doctrine of the established religion, they were, it was claimed, denying the authority of the religion over them.

An interesting and highly important and influential variant of this claim is that heretics cannot be tolerated because they owe primary allegiance to some external authority and therefore cannot be counted upon to acknowledge and uphold the proper authority of the orthodox. To allow them to operate in unmolested fashion would be, therefore, to encourage allegiance to an external authority. Two examples from quite different periods and contexts exhibit this form of argument. First, the major argument used in Great Britain in the sixteenth and seventeenth centuries against tolerating Catholics was that they owed their primary allegiance to the pope and therefore could not be depended upon to support the British authorities.[49] Second, in the United States during the cold war era of the 1950s, it was argued that the Communist party in the United States could not be tolerated because its members owed their primary allegiance to the leaders of the Soviet Union.[50]

A different claim, used particularly with reference to morality, is that deviance cannot be tolerated because it will provide a bad example for others and, in doing so, will undermine authority. Consider some of the opposition to allowing homosexual teachers to retain positions in schools of the United States.[51] The argument is that the presence of these individuals will provide a bad example to impressionable youngsters, who may be encouraged to follow the practice of their instructors, and will therefore undermine allegiance to conventional morality.

A different type of internal threat is to the *unity* of the body in question—unity being considered a necessary condition for survival. Consider, as an example, the arguments of the early

Christian church that doctrinal uniformity was necessary for its continued existence.[52] In contemporary authoritarian nation-states, as a second example, it is often claimed that unity is necessary for survival in the face of a threat by an enemy, whether internal or external. Former President Marcos of the Philippines argued in support of his draconian rule that an intolerant policy toward dissent, and even of diversity of opinion, was necessary in order to meet the dual threats of internal rebellion and economic distress.[53] In South Korea, former President Chun claimed that national unity was required to forestall the threat of aggression from North Korea.[54]

Finally, a commonly perceived threat to the survival of institutions is the loss of *good order* or *harmony* within these bodies. Consider here Burke's contention that, inasmuch as custom and tradition were the foundations of social order, deviations from customary practice could not be tolerated.[55] Consider also the argument, used increasingly by autocratic governments at the present time, that misinformation, harmful information, or simply failure to emphasize information favorable to these governments is disruptive of the social order and cannot, therefore, be tolerated.[56]

The second group of pragmatic arguments concerning tolerating involves several views about the relations between the various segments of society to each other and to the whole. This argument has two forms. According to one, disruption or disunity in one social institution can be expected to spread to others in society or to the society as a whole, in a sort of wave effect.[57] Thus, it may be urged that allowing dissenters to flout authority in the area of religion may lead to a disrespect for authority in the society generally. Or, it may be thought that allowing deviancy in the area of morality will encourage deviancy in other areas, such as politics or business, as well.

The second and historically more prevalent form of this argument is that one sphere of society is more important than the rest for underpinning the authority or unity of society. The most common version of this argument has been the view that good order in the religious sphere is necessary to preserve good order in the political sphere.[58] A second version, one most likely to be voiced at the present time, is the view that good order in the realm of politics is necessary to preserve good order in religion or in morality.[59]

In the area of morality, it has been sometimes argued that a core of common moral belief and practice forms the major part of the cement that must hold any society together. Toleration of moral deviancy, it is then argued, is unacceptable because it will dissolve the bond that unites the parts of society. Both James Fitzjames Stephen, in his response to Mill, and Lord Patrick Devlin, in his response to H. L. A. Hart, made essentially this sort of argument.[60] It is important to note that neither of these writers wishes to make the claim that moral deviancy must be suppressed simply because it is immoral (though it would seem to be a natural argument). They claim, rather, that it must be suppressed because of the harm that it causes for the larger society.

The third and final group of pragmatic arguments is that in which policies of not-tolerating or tolerating are recommended in order to secure some value or attain some goal. Among the most common claims of this sort is that a policy of not-tolerating is necessary to protect the purity of a culture. Thus, Iceland has long had a policy of not-tolerating a variety of things, including the transmission of foreign television programs, in order to protect its unique and homogeneous culture.[61] Similar arguments have been used, with varying degrees of plausibility, in recent years in Japan (regarding the possibility of providing haven for refugees from Indochina), in Australia (also regarding the question of Asian immigration— though with less plausibility than in the case of Japan), and in South Africa (concerning its infamous policy of apartheid).[62]

A different argument of this group is that a policy of not-tolerating is necessary to protect the truth, whether it be religious, political, or scientific. Various religious groups have long argued that correctness of belief can only be preserved against the influence of infidels by intolerance of error.[63] In a similar vein, leaders in Marxist countries have consistently maintained that strict control of the press and other means of communication is necessary in order to preserve correct political doctrine and prevent the intrusion of falsehood, for it is only in this way that the masses can be protected from error.[64]

Distinct from the above examples, however, are famous arguments favoring tolerating as a means of achieving certain values. Perhaps the most famous are those developed by John Stuart Mill. He claimed that policies of tolerating are necessary means of producing diversity, which he valued on several grounds. Apparently he valued it in itself.[65] But he also believed that tolerating in the realms of speech and belief would produce a wide variety of opinions and points of view.[66] Thus far, he is in agreement with the Marxists and various religious sects. But he diverged from them in believing that this diversity is the best means of securing and preserving the truth. In a similar vein, Jean Bodin, among others, argued many years before Mill that a wide variety of religions was necessary and could be achieved only by policies of tolerating. Diversity was valued, not only to determine which religion came closest to truth but also because Bodin believed that each particular religion contained a portion of the truth and that the full truth could only be obtained by allowing a broad spectrum of religions to flourish.[67]

In addition to the arguments about diversity is a class of arguments claiming that policies of tolerating will bring about greater material prosperity. The rationale is that greater prosperity will result from freer trade involving larger numbers of people. Those who are shut out of markets because of religious, moral, or political differences will suffer, but not-toleration will also impoverish a market as a whole by depriving it of significant opportunities for commerce. Historians stress that we should not underestimate the importance of arguments of this sort. For example, it was often claimed by those who favored religious toleration in England during the seventeenth century that toleration would lead to increased trade and prosperity.[68] Their thinking was that markets could be extended and opportunities for trade contacts increased if persons of all religious persuasions felt secure to live and trade in England. Also, they pointed enviously to the example of the Dutch in Amsterdam who were famous as practitioners of religious toleration and who also were prospering mightily in the market.

This sketch of the major groups of arguments concerning toleration is not intended to be complete. But it does include the most important varieties that have been marshaled in the past several hundred years of Western European history. Neither does it attempt to evaluate the arguments or measure their relative strength. Such an effort would require examination of a number of factors that would vary from case to case. In some instances the deciding factors might be matters of fact, as whether a given instance of political dissent does indeed threaten national unity. In other instances the vitality of the arguments might depend on which conceptions of society, of individual nature, and of the relationship between the two are accepted. In yet other cases the crucial factors might be values, whether Mill's value of diversity or the Islamic value of submission to Allah. In succeeding chapters we will examine the application of these arguments in particular and contemporary contexts.

Why Toleration Is Overlooked

7

The Current Scene

It is instructive to contrast the past with the present in the matter of tolerating. Are there, we might ask, reasons to suppose that things have changed so that we tolerate more now than before? There are more people around today and, as a result, we probably have more contacts with others than before. But what does this population increase mean for tolerating? Greater contact certainly increases the opportunity for tolerating one another, but it also increases the opportunity for intoleration and nontoleration. Contact alone seems to cut both ways so that, in the abstract, it is difficult to know what to say. It is not even clear how acceptance is affected by the increased contact we have with our fellow humans due to greater numbers. We might suppose that with more of us around it would be difficult to be as accepting of each other. But, again, greater numbers alone would not seem to change the level of acceptance if, as is true in some nations such as Japan and Iceland, a high level of cultural homogeneity is present.

The increased contact people have with one another is not brought about simply by numbers. Technology has given us greater reach so that we can come into contact with others more readily than before, whatever their numbers. In the past those we had occasion to tolerate or not lived primarily in our local community, but modern production, communication, and transportation often allow our impact on others to reach far beyond our community. This impact is widely felt when power companies produce electricity but, in the process, release chemicals into the air that create acid rain; when politicians talk to millions of people about their political ideas on radio and television; and when individuals with infectious diseases travel from one country to another. But, again, it is not clear whether the greater contact resulting from these factors favors toleration or intoleration. The opportunities for exercising these concepts probably increase with this greater contact, so in that sense these concepts are more likely to be important today than they were in the past. Yet this is not to say that one concept has become more prevalent than the other as the result of these technological changes.

With these changes, however, acceptance may lose its hold to some extent. Technology, in the forms of production, communication, and transportation, does not nurture homogeneity. It is true that some technology creates homogeneity. It does so when we hear the English language spoken nationwide by Dan Rather and when we see the same McDonald's signs not only throughout the United States but throughout the world. Aside from the fact that these forms of homogeneity themselves often need to be tolerated, overall, much technology forces us into more frequent contact with people who are not like us. Those we hear about and see on television, those we meet when we travel, and those with whom we have close encounters of an urban kind frequently neither look nor act like us.[1] It is no wonder that about all we often hope for in such a setting is either toleration or some mild form of nontoleration.

No doubt, the levels of toleration, intoleration, nontoleration, and acceptance have been affected in other ways by changes over the years. As we discovered in chapter 6, the focus of toleration has shifted, for a variety of reasons, from religious to social and political issues and from these to personal issues. But, as we saw, these historical shifts are cumulative. It is not as if when Western societies moved from religious to social and political toleration they lapsed back into their old intolerant religious ways. At least in some respects, then, it would appear that more toleration exists today than did in the past.

Some Reasons for Overlooking Toleration

It is difficult to measure the levels of toleration (and intoleration) people actually exhibit in a way that would allow the confident assertion that they have increased. Still, if we are right about our sociological speculations concerning the contemporary scene, it may be supposed that today, in contrast with the past, we would be more aware and perhaps have more understanding of the family of toleration concepts. If for no other reason, we should have this awareness because we apparently tolerate, are intolerant, and are nontolerant more now than before. But that is not the way it is. It is true that those who live in urban areas believe that they tolerate (and are tolerant) more than their small-town and rural counterparts. Nonetheless, there are several reasons for supposing that these urbanites and people in general are not fully aware of the amount of tolerating they do.

One factor that probably contributes to the lack of awareness as much as any is that our vocabulary for speaking about our actions and reactions to people and to situations is largely dichotomous. We talk about somebody being good or bad, being right or wrong, and having rights or not having them. In contrast, as we have seen, the toleration concepts are trichotomous. Because dichotomous concepts dominate our language when we talk about what it is we should or should not be doing, it is easy to forget about the trichotomous ones.

A second reason for our lack of awareness of the toleration concepts is that we rarely use them when we find ourselves in dilemmas in everyday situations. It is amazing how much tolerating we do on a day-to-day basis and yet how little of it is

101

so labeled. Reflectively monitoring all the tolerating one does in the course of a day is an illuminating exercise. Those living with others probably could give a long list of tolerating occasions even before breakfast is over. The children are behind schedule for school, they are noisy, and they have left a trail of debris in the house from their bedrooms all the way out the door. Somebody has left the television on and husband (wife) is slow to get out of bed.

Our tolerating all these things is only a warm-up for what we must endure the rest of the day. And yet when the day is over, there is a good chance that only a few of the tolerating concepts have been used. There are, of course, substitute expressions. Instead of saying "I tolerate him," the wife might say "I put up with him" or some such thing. But even when taking these ways of speaking into account, a surprising gap remains between the amount of tolerating we do and the amount we talk about. To be sure, a gap always exists between the amount of behavior of one sort or another that we exhibit in our lives and the amount of talk we do about that behavior. Much behavior is, after all, habitual in nature. In moral matters, for example, we perform our duties, and neither we nor others bother even to notice. But there is reason to suppose that we use the toleration expressions even less than we use such expressions as "good," "ought," "morally must," "obligation," "do the right thing," and "have a right."

This reason has to do with the generally reflective role of the toleration expressions in our language. Expressions of toleration and those like "put up with" that act as their surrogates are used more as commentary about what is happening or has happened than as expressions employed to characterize the battle scene of everyday life as it is happening. If someone is talking too much, for example, we are more likely to say "Shut up" than "I cannot tolerate all your prattle." If we so express ourselves, we exhibit intoleration without labeling it as such. It is only later, when we are in a reflective mood, if

we ever are, that we are likely to employ the family of tolera-
tion/not-toleration concepts. Here is another example of the
same point. We may tolerate someone and, in that situation,
express that we are doing so simply by saying, "Oh well, let
her be." It sounds awkward to suggest that what might have
been said is "Let us tolerate her" or something of the sort. In
contrast, on those rare occasions when we are retrospective,
it sounds more natural to say something like "When it comes
to Suzy, we do an awful lot of tolerating, don't we?" This is
not to say that the toleration concepts cannot be used in settings when we are actually tolerating or not-tolerating but,
rather, that we in fact do not do so as often as we might suppose.[2]

But why, in addition to the reflective nature of these concepts, should we employ the family of tolerating concepts so
seldom? At least with respect to the toleration concept itself,
the reasons for tolerating have something to do with our reti-
cence. One of the reasons we discussed in chapter 4 concerns prudence. Because Slim is afraid of Sam, he keeps his
mouth shut. Perhaps Slim never talks about his tolerating Sam
even to himself if it is an embarrassment to him. Likewise we
do not let on what we are up to when we are practicing tactical toleration. We are cool when confronted with Andrew's
anger because, with this response, we figure he will simmer
down faster. This form of toleration is manipulative by definition and thus again, in many contexts, is not likely to be
talked about publicly. No such social reasons exist for remaining silent about procedural toleration, where we tolerate
some behavior while gathering the evidence needed to tell us
what our permanent reactions to that behavior are going to
be. But then this form of toleration is rarer than most. Only in
the case of normative toleration, when we tolerate for moral
reasons, such as to protect other people's rights, are we likely
to be somewhat more comfortable or even proud when talking about how we tolerate others. We will discuss this point
in greater detail later.

The Purification Strategy

Other factors play roles in keeping us from being aware of and perhaps understanding the toleration concepts. Some of these are located on neither the conceptual nor the reason-giving level but instead on the level of argument. People have a tendency to polarize moral issues when discussing them. This tendency prevents them from either discussing or practicing toleration. In part this polarizing is due to the already mentioned dichotomous nature of many of our concepts. Something is claimed to be either right or wrong, and no room is allowed for any in-between options. But the polarizing we have in mind goes beyond that. It has to do with the tendency we find among moral combatants to suppose that their own position is completely right and their opponents' completely wrong. Emotions, our failure to look sympathetically at the other side, our rhetoric, which after a while has a life of its own, and perhaps other factors contribute to this polarization. But even arguments developed in a cool hour can encourage us to move to extremes.

One argument used often enough to deserve a title of its own is the Purification Strategy. The rehabilitative version of this strategy works something like this: First people are depicted as engaging in some intolerated form of behavior—let us say of a sexual sort. Just as the depiction is about to elicit negative responses from us, we are told that no coercion is involved in this stigmatized activity, that those involved have a strong, stable, and loving relationship, and that no deception is present. We can envision here a husband (or wife) with two wives (or husbands) where all of these purified conditions apply—where, as it were, the activity has been rehabilitated. Having been deprived of the usual objections to what is going on, we are further put on the defensive by being asked: "Well what's wrong with such an arrangement?" The final step in applying this strategy is to force us to accept this behavior, by moving us from the extreme response of intoleration, quickly past toleration, all the way over to acceptance.[3]

It takes but little imagination to see how this strategy can be applied to a wide variety of intolerated forms of sexual behavior such as homosexuality, cohabitation, and spouse swapping. With each form, the setting is cleansed of coercion, deceit, and ignorance and is perfumed with love and affection. If those who are intolerant still object by suggesting that the situation is not purified enough, the strategy's open-ended nature allows for additional purification. Thus if the objection is that the spouse swappers will run into trouble identifying which children belong to whom, we can suppose that those involved are infertile or use multiple forms of birth control. Once that is established, then, once again acceptance is demanded by the Purification Strategy.

It would be misleading to suggest that the rehabilitative version of the Purification Strategy is totally misguided. It can serve the useful purpose of reminding us that there may be legitimate exceptions to a rule prohibiting certain forms of behavior. The Purification Strategy, up to the point of asking "And what can be the matter with that?" and receiving a response "Nothing," is perfectly legitimate. It is the leap from this concession to the demand for acceptance where it is not. One reason that the strategy is not legitimate universally is simply that the "that" in "What is the matter with that?" speaks only to the purified form of the behavior in question and not to all its forms. If it is living together that is not tolerated, the Purification Strategy addresses only the purified cases of this behavior form. It certainly does not justify giving blanket approval to the practice itself.

Indeed, in some cases the Purification Strategy does not even have the power to justify giving approval to (be accepting of) the purified cases. One of the weaknesses of this strategy is that purification is often achieved by means of specificity. If purification requires that those participating in the intolerated behavior be rational, informed, and emotionally sound, the strategy may actually apply to very few people. The more purification is required, the fewer people will be covered by it. If, in fact, this is the case, those who might very well have good reasons for being intolerant could feel uncomfortable treating the two groups, the purified and unpurified, so differently. That is, they might feel that they are sending seemingly contradictory signals to the larger society by responding so differently to basically the same form of behavior. Instead, they might think it is better to tolerate rather than accept the purified few while continuing to be intolerant of the vast impure majority. Toleration might be in order as well because in the eyes of a rather conservative general public, although the purified few are doing nothing wrong, they are not doing anything right either. That is, living together in a very purified arrangement might be tolerated, but not accepted, just because it fails to meet some standard (e.g., marriage) that the society accepts as truly being all right.

Of course, if the Purification Strategy applies to more than a few people, the rule mandating intoleration may itself erode to the point that it would make sense to accept the form of behavior that was not tolerated in the past. Thus, in this and perhaps other ways, the strategy could be used justifiably to overthrow an unjustified, intolerant rule. But whether it does or not is not our concern here. What is of concern here is the tendency the Purification Strategy and other ways of arguing have of tempting us to suppose that we *must* accept if we no longer reject some form of behavior. Our point is that the option of toleration, the middle option, should not be automatically overlooked as the Purification Strategy tempts us to do.

What might be called the idealized version of the Purification Strategy also encourages us to overlook toleration. That version works as follows. Some approved form of behavior in the society, such as marriage, is identified. It is then purified or idealized so that it is made to look as good as it can be. This purification makes it easier to say of the purified behavior not only that it is all right but that other options are all wrong. The Contamination Strategy is often used in tandem with idealization. With this strategy, worst-case scenarios portraying the plight of prostitutes, for example, as exploited, used, and abused creatures are presented so as to invite us to be intolerant in the extreme.

Other strategies or arguments yield much the same result as these. Perhaps the most famous is the slippery slope (or wedge) argument where any suggestion that what has been intolerated should now be tolerated is greeted with the thought that once such a process is started it cannot be stopped. With this argument, toleration is not so much overlooked as it is maligned. Once again, this argument has some validity. The particular slope in question may in fact be slippery. But then it may not be, so toleration may turn out to be, as the slippery slope argument suggests it is not, a viable option.

Thus we see that the tendency to overlook toleration as a viable option exists on both sides. Those who are not tolerated may use, among other strategies, the rehabilitative version of the Purification Strategy to leap over toleration to acceptance, while those who are intolerant may use the idealized version of this strategy, the Contamination Strategy, or the slippery slope argument to resist any kind of move in that direction. The result is all-or-nothing thinking. The one side wants it all, while the other wants to give up nothing. Options in between are either forgotten, overlooked, neglected, or quickly passed over.

Response Complexity

We have surmised that today, in contrast with the past, circumstances favoring tolerating *and* not-tolerating probably have increased, while circumstances favoring acceptance have probably decreased. Despite these changes, it does not appear that we talk more about tolerating or not-tolerating. Instead, a variety of reasons seems to be working together to keep us from realizing the nature and extent of these changes. Thus we are perhaps more tolerant today as compared to the past, but we do not talk as if we are. At the same time, we are perhaps more intolerant, but again we do not talk as if we are. This gap between how we act and how we talk about our behavior keeps us from appreciating how important the toleration concepts are to us and also prevents us from fully understanding them.

However, the factors we have examined thus far in this chapter are not all that keep us from understanding these concepts. The inherent complexity of the family of toleration concepts is also a factor. This complexity is manifested in the four basic kinds of reasons for tolerating and not-tolerating (chaps. 3 and 4), in the distinction between the temporary and permanent forms of these concepts (chaps. 3 and 4), and in their varied attitudinal intensity ranging, for toleration, from barely tolerating all the way to near acceptance (chap. 1). But another kind of complexity is present when we tolerate. We will call it *response complexity*. It is concerned with the concrete form of behavior we exhibit when we tolerate or do not tolerate. We can respond in a variety of different ways, and this variety may confuse us when we try to understand whether we are or are not tolerating. Our argument is not that the toleration concepts necessarily suffer from more response complexity than other concepts we employ but, rather, that enough complexity is present when we deploy them to help explain why we overlook and misunderstand them.

It might be thought that response complexity simply is not present when these concepts are deployed. After all, as we have said, tolerating is a matter of *not* doing anything in the face of behavior toward which one has a negative attitude. To put it bluntly, it would seem that response complexity could not possibly be present when one is doing nothing (i.e., not acting). However, this complexity is present—mirrored, as it were, from the side of not-tolerating. It is true that when we tolerate, we do nothing; but doing nothing is always relative to what we could have done. Sally is intolerant of Sam's heavy drinking when she pours his liquor down the drain; and correspondingly she is tolerant when she leaves the stuff in the bottle. She is also intolerant when she speaks sharply to Sam about his drinking or publicly taunts him about it, and, again correspondingly, she is tolerant when she does none of these things. Doing nothing is not a matter of simply doing nothing but of *not* doing this, that, and that, depending on what one could have done. There is, then, as much response complexity in the deployment of the toleration concept as there is with the concepts that we have clustered under the banner of not-toleration. For that reason, and because whatever response complexity associated with toleration is a mirror of what is found on the negative side, we will look at the complexity on the latter side to seek an appreciation of the complexity on the former.

However, before we do, it is worth noting that we have another reason for overlooking the concept of toleration. Inasmuch as the response complexity of this concept expresses itself as an absence of action, as a kind of void, it is not always easy to know when people are tolerating. Is the void of Sally's just sitting there and saying nothing a case of toleration, indifference, or simple failure to note what is going on? She more than likely will know whether she is tolerating, but Sam, in his semistupor, and others who are observing the scene might miss the significance of what is (or is not) taking place.

Turning now to response complexity on the negative side, it is convenient to consider an example taken from international relations, for diplomats seem to understand and thrive on such complexity. The Soviet Union invaded Afghanistan in 1979. Jimmy Carter declared this act intolerable and soon announced that the United States would not participate in the 1980 Moscow Olympics, that there would be a grain embargo, and that other sanctions would be imposed. Simply declaring the invasion intolerable, of course, does not make it so. It might be asked, therefore, apart from his declaration, whether President Carter responded with sufficient determination to warrant saying that the war *was* intolerable to him and his country.

Well, what could he have done? He could have launched nuclear strikes against the Soviet Union either with or without a declaration of war. That certainly would have shown that he did not tolerate the invasion of Afghanistan. Because that might be thought an overreaction, he could instead have launched a worldwide conventional war against the Soviets. Or a lesser response, but one that still might count as a reaction to an intolerable situation, would be to send U.S. troops into Afghanistan. Or, if that were not possible, another option would be to pay for, help supply, and train U.S. client-state troops to do the job.

Not having done any of these things, for whatever good or very good reasons he had, President Carter apparently tolerated the Soviet invasion. He tolerated it by not dropping nuclear bombs on the Soviets, not pursuing a conventional world war, and not sending U.S. or U.S. client-state troops into Afghanistan. Yet while he was apparently tolerating the war in these ways, he still had other options to attempt to show that he and his nation did not tolerate the invasion.

Here are a few of them, beginning with military options. He could have openly sent military equipment to the Mujahideen. Here he had options within options. He could have sent low-tech equipment in small numbers sufficient to do

little more than irritate the Soviets; he could have sent somewhat more equipment but not enough that either side could
win the war; or he could have poured in sufficient advanced
equipment to have given the Mujahideen a chance to win. Or
he could have chosen to blockade the Soviets or to spend
much more money on the American military establishment
to force the Soviets to spend more for their military and, in
that way, bleed their economy to death. Or, moving away
from military responses, he could have cut off whatever aid
the Soviets might have been receiving from the United States
at the time of the invasion, inaugurated boycotts of one or
more commodity that the Soviets needed, stopped cultural
and scientific exchanges, terminated diplomatic exchanges,
boycotted the Soviet Union's allies until they pressured the
Soviets to withdraw, pulled out of the Olympics, or started a
propaganda campaign against the Soviets. To be sure, some
of these responses are not properly those of intoleration but of
nontoleration (i.e., withdrawal). Still, no matter how they get
classified, any lack of a feasible intolerant response would
seemingly count as a tolerant response.

Based on this description of the options available to Jimmy
Carter and, later, to Ronald Reagan, it would seem that the
complexity of the situation would be such that it is almost
impossible to say, overall, whether the United States was or
was not tolerant of the Soviet invasion. It would seem that we
could only say the United States was tolerant in some respects but not in others. If this last view were correct, applying the toleration concepts would indeed be difficult. Although we are arguing that these concepts are not easy to
apply, especially when we might wish to make an overall
assessment, applying them is not impossible. We need consider U.S. policy toward the Soviet invasion of Afghanistan to
be clearly intolerant only if the United States took the most
extreme actions available to it. Dropping nuclear weapons on
the Soviets in response to the invasion would obviously be an

intolerant response. It would also be a nonproportionate response, not to say a foolish one as well.

However, it would be enough for the United States legitimately to claim that it was acting in a minimally intolerant manner if it took steps that might reasonably be thought to lead the Soviets to pull out of that unfortunate nation without, at the same time, generating unreasonable costs to itself and others. In this sense, what counts as tolerant or not is context dependent. In the context of Soviet and U.S. relations, what might minimally count as an intolerant response would involve boycotts, because these are not burdensome and might have some chance of altering the Soviets' conduct. But more likely it would also involve making military equipment in sufficient quantity, and of high enough quality, available to the Mujahideen to give them a realistic chance of encouraging the Soviets to withdraw. So even though applying the toleration concept is difficult because so many options are available, it is still possible to say that, on balance, the United States did or did not tolerate the invasion.

Response complexity exists on the other side of the fence as well. Recall that there are two doors into and out of toleration. We can leave and enter toleration on the negative side or on the positive side (i.e., on the side of acceptance). But acceptance, like its opposites, does not represent a single form of behavior. We accept people and/or their behavior by doing any number of things. What will count as full-bodied acceptance behavior will also be context dependent. On the international scene such acceptance might be expressed by having two nations fuse both geographically and culturally or, short of that, by having one nation actively assist the other in whatever problems it may face. Undoubtedly, under active assistance, much response complexity is present. There are questions not only about how active the assistance program is but also what its nature is. Active assistance in war can mean any number of things, all the way from helping an ally fight the war to merely doing such things as providing intelligence information. When the need is economic, the assistance can be in the form of grants, favorable loans or trade arrangements, and the like.

Full acceptance has some parallels as we move from the international to the personal level. Full acceptance is expressed in the case where Michael, who wants to marry the devoutly Catholic Mary, joins her church and regularly takes part in all its religious ceremonies. Short of that, Michael might avoid joining, but he might still support Mary's wish to raise their children as Catholics and, further, make regular financial contributions to the church. Here we may be unsure of how we wish to describe Michael's responses. If Michael does not become a Catholic, but actively supports the church financially, does he fully accept it or does he *merely* accept it?

In part, the problem is that our behavior on the acceptance side of toleration is not sharply divided into different types in the way it is on the other side. On the negative side, not-tolerating something can mean either being intolerant of it or non-tolerating it, where the former involves making serious attempts to stop the disliked behavior and the latter involves avoiding that behavior. Although response complexity on the acceptance side may be as great as on the not-tolerating side, it does not possess relatively sharp dividing lines to help organize that complexity for us when we talk about it. We simply have no uniform terminology available to use in speaking about these matters. So there is not only plenty of response complexity present on the acceptance side but also a bit of conceptual fuzziness.

This vagueness appears to extend right up to the door leading into toleration. An example highlights the problem. Let us suppose a nation tolerates the noisy and strange religious antics of a group calling itself the Decibelians because it thinks

113

that all groups have rights to freedom of speech and religion. As we have described it, tolerating would involve simply passively allowing this group to act as it wishes (within certain limits no doubt). But if the Decibelians are allowed to act as they do *by right*, then not only do the members of the society have a duty to be passive with respect to them (i.e., tolerate their practices) but somebody within the society also has a different duty actively to protect those rights. We have a kind of paradox then. Apparently, the society cannot tolerate the Decibelians on grounds that they have rights without at the same time accepting them in some sense of that word because it also actively extends protection to them. One can then ask: Is the society practicing toleration here *or* acceptance? It appears to be the former not only because there is passivity with respect to the Decibelian practices but also because the society does not like this particular form of behavior. Yet the society's response appears to be an example of mere acceptance because it takes active steps to protect the Decibelian religious practices from those who might otherwise be intolerant. Indeed, what is more confusing is that those whose duty it is to defend the Decibelian rights against the intolerant in their midst might be barely able to endure all the noisy and strange behavior of these people.

One way to address this paradox is to suggest that "or" in "Is this toleration or acceptance?" need not be understood in an exclusive sense. In this interpretation, the members of the society at large are practicing toleration. They simply put up with the noisy and strange behavior because the Decibelians have rights. Yet, those in charge of guaranteeing these rights, even if they too put up with the same behavior, are not just tolerating. Over and above that, they are practicing a form of acceptance behavior because they are doing something more than nothing. In some respects, then, it can properly be said that the society is exhibiting tolerant *and*, in other respects, acceptance behavior.

There is some plausibility to this interpretation because the question "Is this toleration or acceptance?" need not be answered one way or the other for the society as a whole. Yet, another interpretation makes more sense and runs as follows. The society as a whole is tolerating even though some of its members are actively protecting the rights of the Decibelians. This rights-protecting activity, however diligent it might be, is not necessarily intended to change attitudes toward acceptance—not even from dislike to indifference. Rather, it is in place as an instrument to maintain the tolerant behavior mandated by the rights the Decibelians possess. So although the rights-protecting activity in this example has the appearance of some form of acceptance, simply because it defends the Decibelians, it need not represent acceptance.

Whichever interpretation one prefers, it should be clear by now that enough complexity is inherent in the toleration concept itself and the concepts on either side of it to help explain why it is difficult to understand them and then, in turn, why it is difficult to appreciate how extensively we practice toleration. The complexity also contributes to our failure to appreciate fully how much toleration is actually taking place in various settings. Coupled with various forms of reasoning such as the Purification Strategy and the slippery slope argument, and with the fact that we can speak about our tolerating without explicitly saying that we are tolerating, it becomes even clearer why we fail to appreciate fully the nature of this concept and all the tolerating we do. Finally, leading us down the same path is the unpleasantness of the tolerating process itself. It is unpleasant because two of the major reasons for tolerating suggest that we often tolerate from (embarrassing) weaknesses. Then there is the inherent unpleasantness of all forms of tolerating where we put up with something we simply do not like. Tolerating is by its very nature, it seems, almost intolerable. It is, therefore, not surprising how much effort we put into hiding from others and ourselves how much of it we practice. It is only by covering toleration with a liberal veneer that we come remotely close to accepting it. How that happens, and how even some liberals, the ostensive champions of toleration, misread that concept, is the subject of the next chapter.

Liberalism and Toleration

8

The Relation of Liberalism to Toleration

Political toleration is often thought of as nearly synonymous with liberalism, and previous discussions appear to support this position.[1] As chapter 6 demonstrates, the development of liberalism and toleration in Western Europe is closely linked. What is more, many of the arguments favoring toleration are the products of liberal theoreticians. Governments heavily influenced by the liberal philosophies of Locke or Mill are expected to be tolerant. Many of the pressing social issues of such nations can be framed as questions of what is to be tolerated, whether it be obscenity, drug abuse, or noisy rock concerts.

This picture, however, is far too simple and is distorted in some aspects. As we have seen throughout this study, toleration is not unique to political liberalism, and neither is intolerance foreign to it. Toleration has its proper role in liberalism, but this role is obscured in part by the nature of toleration itself and, in other part, by the nature of the explicit goals that liberals espouse. This chapter, therefore, will be devoted to addressing the twin issues of the particular relation between liberalism and toleration and why this relation is obscure and difficult to understand. It will also canvass the related issue of whether toleration has a proper and important role to play in the concerns of political liberals or whether they would be better served to jettison it altogether.

In a number of ways, it is a misunderstanding to identify toleration closely with Western liberal democracy, inasmuch as all societies mandate tolerating of one stripe or another. In

117

many nations, ethnic and religious minorities are assigned subservient roles and are expected to suffer in silence. Women have been oppressed in nearly all human cultures and, again, have been expected to endure their lot without complaint. And any form of criticism of the government is outlawed in many societies throughout the world. In contrast, toleration of government, of dominant ethnic or religious groups, or of men is widespread and widely acknowledged in these societies.

What sets liberal democracy apart from these other societies is the particular type of toleration it espouses: toleration of the belief, speech, or action of *individuals* by other members of society and by government. Tolerating is as common and unremarkable as air, but instances where powerful social groups tolerate individuals are rare indeed. However, this latter mode of tolerating is more visible and more consequential than others. It is perhaps because of the visible nature of liberal tolerating that the link between tolerating and liberalism seems especially strong. As noted in an earlier chapter, prisoners chained to a wall can intelligibly be said to tolerate their condition, as opposed to accepting, on the one hand, or railing against it, on the other. But from a practical standpoint it hardly matters which course they adopt because these differences in attitude will have little effect. Moreover, it will often be difficult for an observer to determine whether they are tolerating or not. Similarly, a thoroughly weak and oppressed minority may or may not be tolerating, but the practical consequences are likely to be slight. In contrast, a government or an entire society clearly has a wide variety of distinct choices for dealing with solitary individuals, and the selection of one or another of these options will make important differences for the lives of those concerned. So, liberal toleration is more visible than other sorts and may receive greater attention for this reason.

The intersection of liberalism and toleration is complicated by yet another factor. All societies, including the liberal, mandate intoleration of one sort or another. At the very least, any society must be intolerant of murder, thievery, and dishonesty. In addition, any society must be built on a core of shared values, a consensus of what is good and to be sought. Without this consensus, a society will enjoy neither a cohesiveness derived from a shared, common perspective nor a core of agreement on which social policy can be established and disputes should be resolved. The difficulties of the Quebecois in Canada, the Arabs in France, or the Muslim Shi'ite minority in Egypt all serve to illustrate this problem. But values gain definition and significance in contrast to their opposites. A society that values freedom must abhor tyranny. A society that espouses neatness and thriftiness will bewail the untidy and spendthrift. The liberal society can be no different, not only in the sense of demanding adherence to basic standards of decency but in the sense that intoleration will be required in order to vouchsafe the very sort of toleration it requires. If, for example, toleration of individual belief is to be secure, intoleration of attacks on that belief are necessary. Or, if odd, eccentric, or frivolous ways of life are to be tolerated, liberal society must not tolerate violent disruption of them. Liberalism does not eschew intoleration. It requires it, but, again, it is intoleration of a certain sort.

There is another, perhaps surprising, reason for believing that liberal democracies should not be overly closely identified with toleration. It forms no part of the explicit doctrine of political liberalism. The word *toleration* is hardly found in Mill's classic statement of liberalism, *On Liberty*, though 'intolerance' plays a more prominent role.[2] This last point is true despite the importance of Mill's analyses for issues of tolerating. One of the major works of an avowedly liberal stance to have appeared since the Second World War, John Rawls's *A Theory of Justice*, devotes only a few pages to a passing mention of toleration.[3] The reader is unlikely to find a sustained explicit defense or analysis of toleration in the literature of liberalism.

The explanation of this absence is both intriguing and important. Most fundamentally, toleration of the sort that liberalism requires is the dark shadow of the central values that liberals fervently espouse. Liberalism presently comes in so many varieties that it has nearly dissolved as a cohesive political doctrine. There remains, however, a core of values that continue to be identified with it. Among these values are belief in the importance of personal liberty and belief in the intrinsic value of the single human individual. These beliefs clearly intertwine and reenforce one another but are distinct in several ways.

Mill explicitly recognized the necessity of defining the domain of individual freedom and of singling out areas within it that are important enough to require special attention. If, after all, the domain of individual freedom includes only that which can be done while home, alone, with the shades drawn, it could hardly amount to much. Mill wished to establish a general distinction between the protected sphere of individual freedom and conduct legitimately subject to social control. The device he fabricated for this task was his infamous attempt to divide human actions into those that are self-regarding (i.e., affecting primarily the single individual) and those that are other-regarding (i.e., those with significant consequences for others). Critics soon pounced on this distinction and showed how tenuous and difficult to apply it is.[4] Nonetheless, it lives on in subdued fashion in the American legal doctrine of individual privacy, a doctrine that fares only marginally better than Mill's original version.[5] It is easy to see how *any* broad-gauged attempt is likely to be unworkable if viewed as more than a rule of thumb. This feature of being unworkable is due to the problems of determining what acts have consequences only for the solitary individual and the prospect that interference often seems clearly beneficial, even for some types of self-regarding action.

120

Mill was more successful in picking out the areas of belief, speech, and action as essentially private and thus meriting protection. Whether or not Mill's self-regarding/other-regarding distinction is accepted, it is commonly agreed in liberal circles that these private aspects of our lives are particularly important and should be reserved for individual initiative. Other liberals, such as John Rawls, will disagree with Mill's justification of this point but largely accept his conclusions.[6] At any rate, as chapter 6 illustrates, the historical development of liberal doctrine has gradually come to enfold each of these three areas in succession.

Mill argued that people ought to enjoy unrestricted freedom of expression in these areas up to the point at which they cause demonstrable harm to others.[7] Obviously, the threshold of harm with regard to action will be met sooner than that for speech and sooner for both than for belief. Nevertheless, the central point from Mill's perspective and that of his liberal successors is that the burden of proof is on other individuals or society as a whole to demonstrate actual harm. Otherwise, individual liberty is to be unrestricted in these areas. This view of society's burden of proof implies that where, say, individual speech is offensive, silly, misguided, or merely false, it is to be protected unless genuine harm for others can be established. Even where these others have a strong distaste for an individual's expression, they must remain quiescent (in other words, tolerate the speech in question), in service of the value of individual freedom. Thus, from the liberal perspective, toleration is not sought or valued as an end in itself. It is a by-product of securing the individual freedom they cherish, and thus it is readily overlooked because attention is focused elsewhere.

The liberal faith in the value of the individual also has consequences for tolerating, though of a different sort. In many cultures and from many perspectives, certain groups of people are singled out as inherently undeserving of respect or

121

consideration. In classical Athens, non-Greeks were deemed only semihuman, worthy only of slavery or, at best, second-class status as resident aliens in city-states. For much of European history, atheists and non-Christians, as well as professed Christians of the wrong sort, were considered beyond the pale of humane treatment. The caste systems of both India and Japan provided for outcast groups who were not genuine members of the social group and who were considered generally unworthy. The Marxist view of the bourgeoisie is somewhat more complex, but the doctrine clearly implies that it is an inherently tainted class and must be eliminated, often by means of the physical destruction of its members.

There are, in addition, the usual varieties of sexist and racist movements. They share the view that certain groups of human individuals, by virtue of their intrinsic nature, are legitimately the objects of attitudes of disgust, disapproval, and, often, physical abuse. In fact, some bigoted groups would consider it their duty to be intolerant, as some medieval Christians believed they were obliged to persecute heretics and infidels, or some contemporary Marxists, following the lead of Lenin, are persuaded that they must ruthlessly destroy the bourgeois class. For them, some variety of acceptance, or even of toleration, would be at best a weakness and at worst a culpable abrogation of duty.

In contrast to these views, the liberal doctrine of the inherent value of the individual rules out *both* intoleration *and* toleration of the solitary person. It requires something more—namely, full acceptance of that person. However, it must also require, as noted earlier, that some practices, beliefs, or verbal expressions of individuals be legitimate objects of intoleration, or of toleration at best. Of course, it will often be difficult to separate detestation of an individual's particular belief from loathing the individual holding it. This difficulty is nicely illustrated in the recent work of Ronald Dworkin. The basic principle of his liberal position is that of equal concern and respect for all individuals. He carefully argues in defense of affirmative action programs that his principle does not rule out discriminating against particular groups of individuals. It only rules out discriminating against them from certain motives, those of disrespect or loathing, and it rules out discrimination that does not receive its justification by service of some larger social good.[8]

The victims of such programs may take only meager consolation from Dworkin's distinction, but the quandary illustrates the very real problem liberal theory has of reconciling the fundamental principle of individual worth with the necessity of occasionally causing people harm. Furthermore, there will be cases where an individual's beliefs and actions will be so odious, yet so pervade his or her nature, that there seems to be little point in attempting to distinguish affirmation of that person's inherent nature from detestation of the ways in which that nature is expressed. The Adolph Hitlers and Pol Pots of the world appear so thoroughly infused with bigotry and hatred that it stretches credibility to nonetheless claim that they retain an inherent nature, shared with all humans, that requires affirmation. Even the lesser bigots—the contemporary white supremacist J. B. Stoner or his counterpart, the Black Muslim Louis Farrakhan, for example—seem so thoroughly defined by their bigotry that to imagine any remainder worthy of respect seems nearly impossible.

In such cases, even the most determined liberal may have to acknowledge that human nature and the complexity of the human situation may not support affirmation and may, at best, allow toleration. Where people cannot bring themselves to accept others fully, whether because of their offensive nature, because people cannot completely subdue the remnants of their own bigotry, or because they have been so abused that forgetting their past hurt is impossible, tolerating may be required as a second-best alternative. As noted in chapter 1, sometimes attitudes are less tractable and less readily controlled than actions. Where attitudes of acceptance are beyond reach, where the child cannot forget the abuses of the parent or the minority cannot erase the scars of abuses caused by the majority, tolerating may be all that can be humanly asked. Furthermore, in some cases—those where bigotry is not disavowed but reaffirmed, as was the case in South Africa until recently, or where hatred and manipulation continue to be embraced—tolerating may be all that should be given. To seek acceptance or affirmation in such cases may be wrong. Where bigotry and hatred are embraced, the liberal value of the affirmation of the worth of each human individual must become an ideal, a goal to be sought rather than a present guide to action. In such instances, tolerating is the order of the day, even for the most committed liberal.

Thus, in service of its positive value of respect for inherent human worth, liberalism is associated with toleration by ruling out intoleration of a certain sort, that of hatred of individuals as such. It also mandates tolerating of human individuals as a second-best response in cases where the circumstances of human life do not allow full acceptance of the individual person. So, once more, toleration enters the picture only as the negative image of the liberal esteem for individual existence. Once more, it is the positive value that generates enthusiasm and commitment and is the subject of the arguments liberals devise to support their doctrine. But they do not argue *for* toleration. They argue in favor of other, more attractive ideals, and toleration enters by the way.

The Liberal Threat to Toleration

In some respects, however, the characteristic doctrines of liberalism are a continuing challenge to toleration. They challenge toleration not by mandating intoleration but by tending to push attitudes and actions beyond toleration to some variety of acceptance. A hint of this challenge is visible in the previous section, but the issue is sufficiently important to merit further attention. There is a distinct tendency to argue in favor of liberal values by emphasizing the importance of, say, freedom of speech by proclaiming the worth of what is said and encouraging full acceptance of it. It is easy to see why this tendency exists. Those who wish to demonstrate the value of freedom of speech to a skeptical audience are likely to find that the course that promises greatest success is to proceed by showing that good things will follow from it. This emphasis on the positive is particularly true of Mill, the avowed utilitarian, who was constrained by his ethical theory to couch his arguments in terms of good consequences.[9]

When wishing to show the value of freedom of speech, Mill argued that: Allowing a wide variety of opinions to be expressed is more likely to lead to truth than favoring only a few. We can never know whether views that seem quite certainly true today will be demonstrated to be mistaken tomorrow. Few views can be thought to capture the entire truth, but fewer are devoid of truth altogether. It is important to have even clearly false views expressed in order to maintain the vitality of true ones and preserve a vivid sense of why they are correct.[10]

In Mill's pattern of argument the general strategy is to attempt to show that there is something of value, something to admire, even in ideas that seem quite clearly mistaken or silly. In other words, the pressure of Mill's arguments is to push us beyond toleration to acceptance of one variety or another. When arguing in favor of freedom to develop widely divergent ways of life, Mill makes claims of a similar sort. He avows that it is important to have experiments in a variety of ways of life in order to determine which are most worthwhile. Furthermore, people are most likely to develop lives of intrinsic worth if allowed to work them out for themselves. Once more, the pressure of his claims is to push beyond toleration of eccentric, odd, or frivolous ways of life to a view that they

125

surely have some genuine value, even if not readily apparent to the observer.

Mill's critics, Robert Paul Wolff prominent among them, have asserted that Mill's position rests on a number of claims of fact, none of which has any overwhelming prospect of being true. Wolff, though a critic of liberalism in general as well as of Mill in particular, argues that there is a good reason for allowing freedom of speech. But his reason is that it is a requirement of justice and not that good consequences will result.[11] This controversy reveals a curious ambivalence in liberal arguments about freedom. There is a tendency, on one side, to argue on behalf of freedom on grounds that people are likely to do, say, or think good and important things if freedom is secured. Freedom is justified, in other words, by its good consequences. Other liberals, who agree with Wolff on this point, argue that freedoms are based on rights of some sort and that these rights should be vouchsafed whether or not the exercise of them achieves worthwhile results. In this view, if people have the right of freedom of speech, they are entitled to exercise their freedom even if they should do so in silly, obscene, or erroneous ways that have no redeeming qualities. This approach, it would seem, is less likely to push beyond toleration into acceptance.

Both John Rawls and Alan Gewirth have formulated versions of a general argument in which it is claimed that we are morally obligated to grant personal liberty to others on grounds that we wish such liberty for ourselves—and we must wish this liberty in order to fulfill the requirements of our agency as free, rational, individuals.[12] From this perspective there seems to be no requirement that we view the free actions of others as inherently valuable or laudable. We do not, in this view, want freedom for others because we believe it is good. We do not necessarily genuinely wish freedom for them at all. Rather, we are obliged to grant freedom to them in order to secure it for ourselves.

But from the perspective of toleration, there is a difficulty with this view as well. Both Rawls and Gewirth base their defense of freedom on the requirements of free, rational agency—autonomy if you will. Freedom is granted as a requirement of this agency. But this emphasis on autonomy suggests its own limits on toleration, for it is difficult to see how this sort of toleration can extend to acts of irrationality or self-servitude. And it opens the questions of what constitutes the genuine expression of freedom and rationality and who shall make this determination. But, most fundamentally, where expressions *are* determined to be free and rational, there will, once more, be pressure to go beyond tolerating them—to acceptance of one form or another. To determine that a belief or an act is genuinely free and rational is to grant it a considerable accolade, to view it as something to be respected and admired. Mere toleration in this instance would be an inappropriate response.

For another attempt at a workable conception of the relation between liberalism and toleration it is necessary to return to Mill once more. Mill's fundamental aim in *On Liberty* is to free the individual from the tyranny of the majority.[13] In this concern, that of protecting the individual from more powerful groups, Mill is, oddly perhaps, in agreement with his dogged critic Robert Paul Wolff. Wolff's claim is that this protection is a simple requirement of justice, but he does not further elaborate his view.[14] Mill is more forthcoming on these matters in some ways, but the crux of his position lies beneath the surface in others. He argues that where society interferes in the personal affairs of the individual, it will inevitably do more harm than good. This is an implausible view, and Wolff has an easy time producing counterexamples where social interference is clearly beneficial, as in the case of the self-destructive behavior of alcoholism or drug addiction.

Perhaps Mill is being overly heroic on this matter, but elements of his perspective can easily be knit together to produce a more plausible approach. Mill notes that where social groups have the power to engage in extensive interference in individual lives, this power is quite likely to be misused. What is more, as he usefully documents, such central control is likely to erode the qualities of self-reliance, spontaneity, and self-control that he regards as contributing most fundamentally to the value of the individual's existence.[15] The individuality that Mill espouses is of a particular kind, namely, that which includes creativity, self-reliance, and integrity. It is in service of nurturing individuality of this sort that Mill wishes to restrict social interference. This is a conception that may not be congenial to political systems or human cultures where the collectivity is of greater importance than the individual or where the worth of the individual's existence is defined in terms different from Mill's.

Furthermore, Mill's conception of society is of a distinct sort, one where offensive, experimental, or critical activity is not necessarily or inevitably socially harmful. It is a view in which Soviet laws against "slandering the state" would be nearly unintelligible. Mill's view of society is not that of an organic unity held together only when all members submerge themselves to the whole, or a society, like the Japanese, where harmony, cohesiveness, and consensus are the highest values.[16] In such societies free-wheeling, eccentric, or independent individuals *would* constitute a social threat, and, from this perspective, their activities are quite likely to be genuinely harmful to the whole. From Mill's own perspective, however, obnoxious, challenging, or aggressive behavior by individuals does not harm the state. Rather, where society allows such behavior, it is strengthening itself—by supporting the values of individuality that in Mill's view are its highest expression.

With Mill's conceptions of the individual and society, it is natural to view intoleration as only justified in cases of genuine harm to society, where such harm is distinguished from the merely obnoxious or unsettling. Further, where social power and social activism are to be minimized, because of the risk of misuse or to open up space for individual expression, the way is clear for toleration. But it is also clear that tolerating is threatened by this approach as well. For, if society really is strengthened by challenge, there are grounds for not just tolerating but encouraging and appreciating it. Mill's arguments are useful in supporting the position that it is a good idea to limit the power that society has to manipulate the individual, but the pressure, once more, is to push beyond toleration to acceptance. Liberal arguments seem better suited for fending off intoleration of certain kinds than for a persuasive defense of toleration itself.

So the question remains, why should toleration remain a feature of the liberal society? In fact, some very good reasons exist for believing that liberal societies would be better off by seeking to eliminate it.

The Importance of Tolerating for Liberal Societies

The repugnant nature of tolerating has been carefully documented in this work. By definition, it goes against the grain. It is contrary to what people are inclined to do and is by its nature unpleasant. But this repugnance is not suffered only by those who tolerate, who choose to endure what is offensive to them. The groups or individuals who are tolerated will be nearly as distressed (as was noted in chap. 3). Being tolerated is no doubt preferable to being subject to intoleration, but it is still not the way most people would wish to be treated. To be tolerated is, after all, to be the object of attitudes of disapproval or contempt. It includes the recognition that the persons holding such negative attitudes would, other things being equal, prefer to act in accordance with them. Particularly where those tolerated are weak or small in number, a continuing sense of vulnerability will exist as they recognize that toleration could always explode into something else.

But those who are tolerated have other reasons to be upset with their lot. It is natural for people to wish to be accepted or receive approval. They naturally wish for others to hold them in esteem rather than be the objects of reined-in contempt. There would seem, in addition, to be strong doctrinal support within liberalism for such attitudes, for the core of the liberal credo is the appreciation of the worth of the individual.

What is more, substantive reasons exist for believing that liberal doctrine readily allows societies to be cleansed of toleration. One of the pervasive themes of this chapter is that the pressure of liberal principles and arguments is to push attitudes beyond toleration and toward acceptance and approval. From this perspective it would seem to be an easy matter to educate members of liberal societies to appreciate the genuine value of odd or unsettling behavior or to understand how what appears offensive to them actually contributes to strengthened personal character and aids in the development of a vivacious, spontaneous, and independent society. With this orientation, liberals would be well positioned to view instances of tolerating as unfortunate, as resulting from irrational quirks that the individual should attempt to overcome or as a consequence of a failure to understand clearly the implications of liberal doctrine. Tolerating would then come to be viewed as an unfortunate lapse from which individuals should attempt to escape or as something that itself should be tolerated in those sad instances where individuals are unable to cure themselves. It is quite plausible, therefore, to believe that societies should not resist the pressure of liberal arguments, should work to remove toleration from their midst, and should make the effort to establish something better.

There are, however, good and important reasons for wishing to retain the prickly and uncomfortable concept of toleration in the liberal pantheon. A basic consideration is that it serves the important function of safeguarding the very values of freedom and individual worth that are so beguiling to the liberal perspective. Toleration deserves attention because freedom and individual worth require that society sometimes tolerate that which seems genuinely to be of no value or even worse than no value. All too often in contemporary society, it is thought sufficient to demonstrate that a given activity or set of beliefs is of no value in order to justify the conclusion that it lies beyond the sphere of freedom.

This is a kind of argument understood very well by activists in the American Civil Liberties Union, who are often busy working on behalf of pornographers, the Nazi party, or the Ku Klux Klan. They argue that, genuinely despicable and worthless though these groups may be, respect for freedom and individual worth requires tolerating *even them*. If, in other words, the pressures of liberal arguments are accepted, and people look for something of value in all points of view and modes of life, they may become disillusioned with liberalism when they can find nothing to admire in certain groups. They may feel that they have been misled by liberal theory, or they may continue to accept the liberal perspective but come to believe that they have found legitimate exceptions to general liberal policies of toleration. They will be correct, of course, in believing that legitimate exceptions exist. It has been pointed out that even liberal societies require some intoleration. But retaining and emphasizing the idea of toleration serve as important safeguards by conditioning members of liberal societies to the notion that even that which is offensive and seemingly without value may require patient endurance. When intoleration is justified, it must be for the correct reasons and not simply because people are offended and can find nothing of worth.

131

In the same vein, but from a different perspective, tolerating performs the important function of allowing a third social response, mediating between acceptance and intolerant suppression. Explicitly introducing the idea of toleration into contemporary discourse, along with education in its mode of use, could be quite helpful in coming to terms with a number of emotionally laden issues contemporary societies must face. It is important that people understand, for example, that granting rights to homosexuals need only be toleration, not acceptance or endorsement of their way of life.

In such cases it is particularly important to recognize that toleration does not require changing one's own values or adopting the norms of those tolerated. Mill would have been the first to insist that people should have distinct values and hold to them with fervor. But he should also have explicitly acknowledged that where values are fervently held people will be unsettled when they encounter values different from their own or when they feel threatened by alien beliefs. Furthermore, living together as one democratic nation requires that one set of laws govern the whole and that people may find themselves outvoted or overruled in cases where values and beliefs clash. Where people recognize that they have toleration as an option, they may be able to compromise or accept defeat on such matters without feeling that they have betrayed their own values by doing so.

It would be quite useful in the current controversies over abortion, patenting of life forms, genetic engineering, animal rights, or the death penalty for advocates on both sides of these issues to recognize that, if they are on the losing side, they need not sacrifice their values in order to accommodate the solution the larger community has adopted. They may recognize that they need not bomb abortion clinics or attempt to sabotage scientific experiments in order to feel they have not compromised themselves. The recognition that toleration is an option will not suffice, in itself, to resolve these issues, but it may certainly prove useful as one instrument among others in attempting to achieve a workable resolution of them.

In a utopian society where mutual human understanding was complete, or where there was no jostling or friction among differing groups, or where people never narrowly pursued their own interests to the exclusion of others, *or* where narrowly doctrinaire and intolerant groups did not continually spring into existence, the useful option of toleration might be unnecessary. But that is not the world we inhabit.

Of course, as pointed out elsewhere, a recognition of the value of toleration in an imperfect world may not serve as much solace to those who are tolerated. They will naturally wish for their values—and for themselves—to be understood and appreciated and will seek wholehearted respect and approval insofar as they are able. But, even here, for those too weak, too odd, or too frivolous to gain such respect, toleration serves as a necessary safeguard. Groups such as these may not have the resources to achieve acceptance in society. For them, toleration may be the only alternative to intoleration. It may be an option they are able to achieve where more desirable ones are not within reach. And gaining toleration may serve as a way station to a more desirable situation in the future, as in the United States the Irish or Greeks have been able to move from the tolerated fringes of society to positions of much greater stature. For such groups toleration is not ideal, but it is better than nothing and better than what they might be able to achieve without having it as an option. And, in the nonideal world, these will sometimes be the best options that are practically available.

The story of this chapter is that toleration is neither as uniquely nor as closely associated with Western liberalism as has been commonly believed. It has a role to play, and an important one, but its very nature is to be reclusive and

133

readily overlooked. Its importance is best appreciated if it is grouped with meliorating concepts, such as compromise, patience, or restraint. These would not be included in the values of a perfect society but play important roles in spreading humanity and decency in the fractious world we have. Freedom, human dignity, and creativity are valued for themselves and would be sought even in utopian societies. The nature and role of meliorating concepts are different. They are not valued in themselves but for their utility in improving imperfect lives in an imperfect world. Toleration is to be found among them.

Ideological Controversy

The Marxist Challenge

Liberalism and its concomitant theory of toleration have received their most straightforward and thoroughgoing attack from a Marxist of the Frankfort School, Herbert Marcuse. Although Marcuse's version of Marxism is revisionist in a number of aspects, his many-pronged attack on liberal toleration is representative of Marxist theory and can therefore be used profitably in further exploring the relationship between toleration and liberalism.

First, Marcuse says of toleration what Marxists generally say about freedom and democracy, namely, that they are important and valuable but cannot be achieved in any genuine manner under present social conditions. Rather, radical social and political transformation must occur before they can be realized for all in unalloyed form. Second, in common with usual Marxist procedure, Marcuse acknowledges that liberal societies contain a type of toleration, as they embody a sort of freedom and a sort of democracy. He argues, however, that the social conditions of liberal, capitalist society work to transform toleration from a liberating force into another instrument of repression.[1]

The toleration that exists in present-day liberal societies is called "pure" or "abstract" by Marcuse. "Pure toleration" is simply the practice of allowing groups or individuals to express themselves in whatever manner they please, so long as they remain within the bounds of the law and do not attempt to stifle the views or interests of others (p. 85). Pure toleration in itself seems to be unexceptional and even admirable.

135

Marcuse claims, though, that under the conditions of present-day society, this toleration is an instrument of repression. It is repressive because of what he calls the "background conditions" of society. The most important of these conditions are: (a) the control by the predominant forces within society of the institutional forms of physical violence (i.e., for Marcuse, police and army forces, prisons, mental institutions, and hospitals) and (b) the simple predominant situation of the ruling (or majority) classes. Under these conditions, toleration is repressive. While dissidents, the voices of minority, or repressed groups are not actually stifled, they cannot effect actual social change due to the presence of these social background conditions (p. 85). Thus, toleration is a sham and functions merely as a means for venting discontent while ensuring the preservation of the status quo.[2]

To his credit, Marcuse is specific about the ways in which liberal toleration performs this repressive function. He notes that the traditional liberal defense of toleration depends upon a fundamental premise. Toleration, he claims, is justified according to liberal theory because it leads to truth. However, it can lead to truth, on this theory, only if the masses of people can examine the various views and claims presented to them in a reasoned and objective manner. If people critically examine various propositions presented to them, then there is no reason to believe that they will not separate the true and progressive from the false and reactionary (pp. 89–90, 95).

But Marcuse rejects this liberal defense of toleration. He argues that, because of the insidious effects of the social background conditions, the masses will be predisposed to accept the views and interpretations that serve the interests of the established powers and to reject the views that undermine the strength of the status quo. For example, Marcuse claims that if people are presented with two equally reasonable and balanced articles on the FBI, one supporting it and one opposed to it, they will be predisposed to accept the favorable article and reject or ignore the unfavorable one (p. 98).

136

Unfortunately, Marcuse does not explain exactly what the nature of this predisposition is or how the dominant social powers come to establish and preserve this bias. He may believe that people have a simple psychological tendency to favor whatever supports the status quo and to distrust whatever is critical of it (p. 98). However, at times he appears to favor more exotic explanations, such as the view that bias is built into the very structure of our language and values (p. 96). At other times he hints that the dominant powers of society provide the masses with a biased interpretative framework of concepts and perceptions (pp. 95–98). On yet other occasions, he says simply that there is a continual background chatter of commercials, political speeches, traditions, commemorative holidays, and the like that all serve to bolster conventional attitudes on the emotive level (p. 119).

It may be that Marcuse believes that all these differing factors serve to bias the views of the ordinary people and to prevent them from assessing information and opinion in a rational and objective manner. However, his claim here cannot be adequately assessed without a systematic understanding of his views. It is important to possess this understanding, for Marcuse wishes to make the very strong additional claim that these factors not only make rational assessment more difficult but in fact make objectivity impossible (pp. 87, 95, 96). His theory carries a heavy burden of proof at this point, particularly inasmuch as he believes that objective assessment is possible for *some* human beings. The highly educated academic elite can escape subjectivity (pp. 120–23).[3] Only the masses and the nonintellectuals are unable to effect such an escape.

Because the masses cannot be moved from their passive acceptance of the dominant ideology by means of appeals to reason and fact, dissidents can only hope to alter mass opinion by relying upon the same techniques of persuasion that are employed by the dominant powers. That is, radicals can hope to gain a hearing for themselves within the limits of lib-

137

eral society only through use of the same techniques of mass advertising, subtly slanted television programs and documentaries, and massive public events that are used by the dominant opinion makers in liberal society. Yet, as Marcuse points out, no dissident groups have access to the resources (e.g., money, skilled personnel, communications networks, etc.) that could enable them to present their positions effectively. Once again, ostensible toleration results in subtle repression. Dissidents are not prevented from voicing their beliefs, but they are, by the nature of social conditions, denied access to the means of effectively altering mass belief (pp. 117–20).

Finally, liberal toleration is repressive, according to Marcuse, by allowing the most base, hate-filled, and offensive opinions, such as those of the Nazis, the KKK, and certain religious fundamentalists, to circulate just as freely as those expressed by progressives. The result is a cacophonous mixture of the good with the bad that subtly convinces people that progressive and nonprogressive views have the same value. A further result is that the liberating potential of progressive views is blunted, thereby permitting the repressive forces of the status quo to work unmolested upon the society (pp. 85, 94, 97–98, 120).

Thus far only the portion of Marcuse's argument has been presented that explains the ways a policy of liberal toleration prevents dissent from bringing about social change. What is still needed is Marcuse's account of why preventing effective dissent is actually repressive. That is, why does it matter that small groups with views differing from the majority cannot affect the views of that majority? After all, if these small groups are permitted to voice their views, what grounds do they have for complaint?

Marcuse presupposes throughout his essay that an effective presentation of dissident views does not mean simply that they are presented well enough so that they *might* persuade the masses. It means, rather, that they are presented in such a way that they *actually* alter the views of the masses and in so doing help to bring about radical social change (pp. 109–10).

How can Marcuse reasonably hold to such a presupposition? His implicit answer is that the existence of violence and represssion is an objective fact that does not depend upon particular values for its veracity (pp. 87, 101, 103, 105, 120). It stands alone to be seen and understood by all. Furthermore, he claims as objective fact that the views of the Left support liberation while those of the Right nurture repression and violence. Therefore, to fail to ensure the success of leftist reforms and movements is tantamount to allowing suppression to continue (p. 111). To fail to use every means to ensure that policies of the Right are defeated is also tantamount to supporting repression and violence.

Because Marcuse has avowed that the policies of liberal toleration prevent both the success of leftist programs and the defeat of those of the Right, they serve to ensure that repression continues. This outcome of the policies of liberal toleration explains why, for Marcuse, it is a mistake to be sanguine about the failure of the dissident Left to gain support for its views and why there should be concern when it cannot effect social change. Though Marcuse agrees that toleration is a valuable ideal, he argues that it is less important than the eradication of suffering and violence and therefore must give way before policies that will effect the elimination of these evils (p. 110). For this reason, Marcuse claims that intolerant policies toward rightist views and policies must be practiced. He presumes that intolerant action as well as intolerant speech is justified, and even necessary, to vouchsafe the success of the leftist program.

This intoleration will ensure the effectiveness of leftist dissent in the following ways. First, by providing a strong and intolerant attack on the views of the status quo, Marcuse hopes to jolt the masses out of their apathy and passivity. He does not, apparently, entertain any hope that such a jolt will

139

make them any more objective or rational. It will only open a space so that their attitudes may swing from the center or right to the left (p. 112). Second, by engaging in spectacular acts of violence or lawlessness, by refusing to give opposing speakers a hearing, and by in fact attempting to silence and thwart them in various ways, Marcuse hopes to overcome the disadvantages that plague the small and impecunious Left (pp. 118–19). The Left may not be able to buy the television time it needs to attempt to sway the opinion of the masses, but it can get itself on the airways for free by engaging in violent and spectacular action. Finally, by demonstrating their contempt for the repressive views of the Right, dissidents hope to overcome the false value neutrality implicit in the larger society's policies of liberal toleration (pp. 119–20). That is, by introducing value charges into mass consciousness, Marcuse believes that dissidents can undermine the effectiveness of liberal toleration and thereby undermine the status quo as well.

The Liberal Response

Because the liberal ideology is so varied, it would be surprising if liberal responses to Marcuse were not varied. Nonetheless, it is possible to outline certain general features of how liberals might respond to Marcuse's attack on their ideology and, in the process, show how he, like many others, has managed to misunderstand the family of toleration concepts.

The portrait of the liberal response to Marcuse can begin by noting some areas of agreement with him. They can agree that in present-day society average people do not give careful attention to important issues, are lethargic, and tend to support the status quo unthinkingly. Indeed, liberals from the time of Mill have been persistent critics of mass culture and have worked hard to overcome the intellectual lethargy of ordinary people. Liberals can also acknowledge that it is difficult for dissident or minority groups to present their views to the masses effectively, although this truism hardly applies only to the dissidents from the Left. Finally, liberals partly agree with Marcuse's claim that the mass media's jumbled presentation of the trivial alongside the vitally important makes it difficult for people to distinguish the two.

While they can agree that there is merit in Marcuse's criticism of present-day liberal society, it is likely that liberals would fault Marcuse's arguments and fault his conclusion that policies of intoleration are the best means of dealing with these deficiencies. In addition, liberals would likely argue that Marcuse has misunderstood the correct nature of toleration in various ways and that his misunderstanding further undermines his analysis.

Perhaps the most fundamental difficulty in Marcuse's position, from the liberal point of view, is in the tension (one is tempted to call it a contradiction) between two fundamental premises of his argument. He holds both that: (a) the average person cannot alter his or her bias in favor of the status quo and that (b) it can be known clearly and objectively that rightist or moderate views either support or sustain repression and that leftist views nurture liberation.

But why should it be so difficult for the average person to appreciate the truth of the leftist position if it is so clearly and objectively true? Average people are surely able to appreciate and respond to many types of factual and objective information that often undermine or weaken the authority of the dominant powers. For example, they can understand that economic conditions are difficult. They can see that people are out of work, and they can tell when they lack sufficient resources to feed and clothe themselves and their families. They can tell when public services, such as education, medical services, and transportation systems, are not being provided adequately and efficiently. Furthermore, despite the best efforts of governmental and business leaders, they often respond actively to these conditions. Politicians are sometimes turned out of office, approval of public figures declines in polls, people lodge complaints against governments or businesses that are serving them poorly, and, finally, they occasionally organize into groups to press their complaints and work for change.

If the views of the leftists are objective in the sense that they are based on factual information, it would appear to liberals that Marcuse is simply mistaken in arguing that average people cannot understand or respond to them. There is, rather, considerable evidence that the case is otherwise and that the best efforts of government and business are insufficient to prevent citizens from reacting to those conditions that are of interest and concern to them.

The liberal faith in the value and autonomy of the individual requires that people ultimately be able to shape their lives and values independently of social pressures. Liberals from John Stuart Mill to John Rawls would acknowledge that individuals are in a constant battle to keep from being overwhelmed by social pressures. They are likely to make use of the claims of the preceding paragraphs to support this contention. Where they fundamentally diverge from Marcuse is in their faith that ordinary people have the resources to conduct this battle effectively. Marcuse must deny that ordinary people can resist social pressures and must, therefore, give the central role to an elite few, the vanguard of the proletariat. The core of the liberal view is that individuals must ultimately liberate themselves. For Marcuse this self-liberation is impossible. They must be granted their liberation by a select cadre.

Perhaps Marcuse would respond that the truths of political philosophy, though objective and uncontroversial, are abstract and difficult to grasp, particularly for those with limited education. His claim, that is, may be that the objective truths that concern him are theoretical rather than factual (pp. 87–88, 122), and, therefore, they may resemble truths of the physical sciences that are objective and based on reason but are none-theless often quite abstract and difficult to grasp. This sugges-tion would seem a plausible interpretation of Marcuse's position for it reinforces his view (and the view of Marxists in general) that the leftist views are based on science, and it would also explain why he believes that the core of the leftist movement must be composed of a highly educated and ratio-nal few. Such material, because of its abstractness and diffi-culty, could easily be manipulated and distorted in such a way that the masses, particularly those with little education, could be readily misled by the ruling elite.

The liberal response to this interpretation would be to claim that average persons can be educated to understand the basic truths of physical science and that various books per-form the job of laying out these truths for the general public quite adequately. Once these truths are understood, there is little reason why ordinary people's understanding of them would be easily manipulated by speeches and propaganda. If Marcuse's political theories are indeed similar to the basic theories of the physical sciences, there is no reason why the mass of people could not be educated to understand them in the same way. A mainstay of liberal ideology is that educa-tion is the means necessary for people to gain control of their lives. It is no accident that liberals as diverse as John Locke, John Stuart Mill, John Dewey, and John Rawls have written about education and emphasized its importance for indi-vidual freedom and for sustaining liberal democracy.

It could be argued that liberals are mistaken on this matter and that average persons could never be educated to under-stand the truths of Marcuse's political theories. But, if this defect of ordinary people cannot be remedied, the conse-quences for Marcuse's position are even worse. He would then be forced to admit that the inability of average persons to grasp his theories is due to the inherent limitations of their own understanding and not to the difficulties posed by the

143

social structure. The reason average persons have difficulty grasping the abstract truths of the physical sciences is because of the intrinsic difficulty of the material itself, and this difficulty would not be lessened if the social structure changed. There is no reason, that is, to believe that the truths of physics are any easier for citizens of socialist countries to understand than they are for citizens of capitalist countries. So if the truths of political philosophy are like the truths of the natural sciences, then any difficulty that people have in understanding them can be traced to the inherent difficulty of the material itself and not to the distortion of social conditions.

Marcuse would no doubt respond to this point by claiming, once more, that the problem *is* a social one because people have been systematically miseducated and misled by dominant social forces. But for liberals this claim simply changes the issue. The reason misinformed and miseducated people do not know the truth is that they have been deceived, not that they are incapable of knowing the truth. It is quite possible that average persons are misinformed and even miseducated about the issues of political philosophy, but these deficiencies do not entail that they are incapable of understanding such issues. What is more, a condition of being misinformed or receiving a distorted education can easily be corrected—by providing correct information or reeducation.

To be completely fair to Marcuse, however, we should note that he has another avenue of explanation open to him. Marcuse, and the Marxists generally, tend to use terms such as *repression, suppression,* and *violence* in a very broad and specialized way. These terms do not refer to particular acts or events but to the overall structure of society and to its manner of functioning. To grasp their meaning, it is necessary to grasp an entirely new framework of interpretation, one quite different from that found in liberal politics. It is easy to imagine and appreciate that such a shift in basic perspective would

144

not be easy either intellectually or psychologically. One can also imagine, as Marcuse seems to state at one point, that it would be nearly impossible for the average individual, lacking education, struggling to earn a living, and bombarded by social pressures, to accomplish such a difficult feat of reorientation (p. 113). Yet it is also understandable that, if society were to undergo a fundamental and radical transformation, the average person, caught up in the change, would be able to accomplish the paradigm shift much more readily. And, if the new paradigm were one of liberation, it would be easy to believe that these individuals would then become "genuinely free" and a "purely democratic society" would be established.

The difficulty with this interpretation is that, if it is correct, it gives Marcuse's game away because the notions of pure, context-free rationality and objectivity suddenly disappear. *Within* the leftist perspective, it may be quite clear that leftist policies are liberating and rightist policies repressive. But within the rightist paradigm, it may be equally clear that the opposite is the case, as many rightist thinkers can cogently argue. In other words, on this interpretation, there could be no neutral perspective from which one could make a rational and objective decision to shift from one perspective to the other.

The juxtaposition of Marcuse's two presuppositions results in a painful dilemma for him. Under several plausible interpretations of what it might mean to say that the views of the Left are objective and reasonable, Marcuse's argument that people cannot alter their biased views fails. On the other hand, under a plausible theory of why people cannot alter their political views, Marcuse's claims to objectivity must be abandoned.

The above are internal criticisms of Marcuse's position. From a liberal perspective, important external criticisms may also be made. Liberals certainly join Marcuse in valuing an

145

ideal of human life in which individuals act freely and rationally, autonomously if you will. They further agree that the great mass of human life falls short of achieving this ideal. However, liberals part ways with Marcuse on the question of how to go about approaching this ideal more closely. Marcuse quotes Mill—the "true" liberal he says—approvingly on this matter. Mill, he notes, states that not all people are ready or equipped to enjoy freedom and its attendant autonomy (pp. 86, 93, 106). They can only be given freedom when they can properly make use of it. Ignoring, for the moment, the fact that Mill intended this limitation of freedom as a justification of British colonial policies (which, it may be presumed, Marcuse would not have applauded), Marcuse glosses Mill's claim as meaning that human beings cannot enjoy freedom until social conditions are right. That is, they must subject themselves to enlightened leadership until such a time as conditions are right for them to be freed (p. 105).

To this reference to Mill, present-day liberals would add another, namely that the only way for human beings to become truly free and rational is by exercising their capacities for free and rational activity.[4] In the same way that one learns to walk by developing and exercising that capacity, so one becomes free by exercising and developing that capacity. Liberals cannot, of course, conclusively prove this point of Mill's, any more than Marcuse can prove his contention that human beings can only become free by exchanging one set of masters for another. However, they would find it strange that one should attempt to become free by remaining unfree, and when recent history is examined (e.g., the experiences of former colonies once cut loose from their colonizers) liberals can plausibly argue that their perspective on these matters finds greater confirmation than does Marcuse's. (At present liberals can also point to the struggles of former East Bloc nations to achieve genuine democratic freedom rather than simply exchanging one oligarchy for another. These nations are

146

convinced that they can only achieve freedom by seeking to exercise it and preserve it for all citizens, not by putting themselves under the tutelage of another "vanguard.")

Liberals are also likely to find Marcuse's views dangerous. While they have greater faith than he does in the ability of average human beings to enjoy lives of freedom and rationality, they have less faith in the wisdom and goodwill of a small cadre of leaders and in the capacity of such cadres to lead society to greater freedom (even if these leaders are the rational and enlightened elite of which Marcuse speaks). Once more, liberals cannot conclusively prove their views on these matters—or disprove Marcuse's—though they are likely to believe that the events of this century (particularly the events in those Marxist countries that broadly share Marcuse's political philosophy) more closely support their perspective than his.

Although, then, liberals cannot conclusively prove that their views are correct or that Marcuse's view is mistaken, the argument between them has not been fought to a draw. The liberals can easily argue that Marcuse has a heavier burden of proof to carry than they do. Acceptance of his position entails withdrawal of the rights of freedom of speech, an action that involves being actively intolerant of those who disagree with the leftist position. As he acknowledges, such actions lead to grave consequences and, therefore, liberals might well say, should be avoided unless they are necessary to avoid even greater evil (pp. 109–10). The consequences of the liberal position, on the other hand, are that rights are strengthened and toleration nurtured. For those who value rights and toleration, as Marcuse claims to do, the burden of proof should rest with those who wish to withdraw these values. Because Marcuse can at best claim only that he has not been conclusively refuted, liberals could conclude that he has not met his burden of proof and that he has not justified withdrawing toleration and the rights of freedom of speech.

Yet, even if democracy and freedom were realized in fragmentary and distorted form in contemporary societies, and if toleration often served only to buttress the status quo, liberals are likely to claim that it would be a grave mistake to defer the pursuit of these ideals to a remote utopian future (as does Marcuse, pp. 81, 82, 104–05). To follow such a course is to risk abandoning them altogether. In particular, however, deferring the practice of toleration to a utopian society rests upon a mistaken understanding of toleration itself.

This claim about the error of deferring the practice of toleration brings the defenders of a liberal position to the final area of criticism of Marcuse. Marcuse's view of the sort of society in which genuine toleration exists is not clearly explained by him. He does say that it is a society in which all individuals would be equals and in which no repression or violence would exist (pp. 82, 84). Presumably, it would also be a society in which full freedom and genuine democracy would be realized. The difficulty with this view, for liberals, is that there would be no place in such a society for toleration because there would be nothing to tolerate. As we have insisted throughout this book, people only tolerate something or someone when they have a negative attitude toward it yet put up with or endure the object of their disfavor. Toleration can exist only in an imperfect world of conflict and frustration. It is something that enables human beings to live gracefully and with respect despite the irritations of their social existence. Toleration is important in the liberal perspective just because of the world's imperfect nature.

Liberals are apt to contend that one of the strengths of their position is that it is designed to help people live humanely in a less than perfect world filled with less than perfect people. Part of the difficulty with Marcuse's view is that he has apparently not realized this feature of the liberal position. However, by being discontent with a less than perfect world, Marcuse has developed a set of views that possesses the danger of transforming the world into an even less hospitable place than it already is. Another difficulty is that he appears to presume that a world free of repression and violence (i.e., a world free of *one* kind of intoleration) will automatically be a tolerant one (p. 82). This is a misguided view. Toleration is not simply the mirror image of intoleration. The concept, and the social world, are far more complex than that.

Perhaps the most fundamental difficulty with Marcuse's understanding of toleration, from the liberal perspective, results from the very nature of his political philosophy. He is an absolutist. He is quite sure that his position is objectively true and that all others are false. This fact in itself need not result in a rejection of toleration. Religious groups share the same sort of certainty and yet many of them have come to acknowledge the importance of toleration. What distinguishes Marcuse's position is his conviction that only the views of the Left can lead to liberation while all others result in or nurture repression and violence. Therefore, only the views of the Left can be supported (pp. 107, 109, 119–20). All others must be fought. But toleration is melioristic. It lies on the middle ground between acceptance and complete intoleration. For Marcuse there clearly can be no such middle ground. One's views are either correct, in which case they should be accepted; or one's views are wrong, in which case they must be destroyed. Because of this dichotomous thinking, it would appear to be impossible for Marcuse to develop a genuine theory of toleration—even though he may want to borrow its aura for his own purposes.

Conclusion

Marcuse is not alone in wishing for a perfect world. This desire is as natural as rain. He shares the human urge to be free from irritation, frustration, and injustice. There is no harm in that. However, his desire for a perfect world prompts him to overlook the importance of toleration in the world that exists and to fail to understand that any actual world is likely to require toleration in order to preserve human freedom and allow a humane response to the inevitable frustrations of ordinary life.

He also shares with others the tendency to dichotomize the world into good and bad, right and wrong, or Left and Right. For him there can be no middle ground, no room for compromise or for toleration. Politics is a Manichaean battle between freedom (in his sense) and repression. Whoever is not uncompromisingly battling for freedom is, in one way or another, in service of repression.

This tendency to dichotomize infects even the liberal position, as was seen in the previous chapter. Even liberals are prone to push arguments in support of freedom beyond toleration into acceptance. Preserving the essential tension of toleration, the tension between dislike and restraint, is difficult even within the ideology most closely identified with it. In this light, it is not surprising that toleration and its importance easily escape notice in ordinary life and among ordinary people.

But the lesson of these past few chapters is not simply that toleration is easily overlooked. It is, in addition, that a variety of powerful forces is continually at work to push it from view. And the problem is exacerbated by the nature of toleration itself. It is the Ugly Duckling of liberal ideals: prickly, elusive, and repellent. Yet, because of its role in preserving freedom, protecting the downtrodden, and sustaining democracy, it is tremendously important all the same.

Concluding Comments

Importance of Toleration

We noted at the beginning of this study that the concept of toleration has for the most part been overlooked by philosophers and political theorists. As a result of our examination of this concept, and the cluster of concepts related to it, we can now see why toleration is so elusive. One of the many reasons we uncovered is that toleration is not exciting in the way liberty, freedom, equality, justice, and fraternity are. It does not impel us to create revolutionary slogans or make righteous demands. No one has stirred a crowd with the slogan "Give me tolerance or give me death." Toleration is evidently made of lesser stuff. It is associated with compromise, concession, hesitation, and patience along with aggravation and frustration. It is positively uninspiring and, as a result, seemingly uninteresting and unimportant.

Toleration is also seemingly uninteresting and unimportant for a totally different reason. It is not a morally pivotal concept in the sense that no moral principle is generated and no moral system created simply by understanding it. Instead, engaging in normative ethics on any level—personal, community, national, international—requires appeal to moral principles that apparently have little or nothing directly to do with toleration. The moral recommendations people issue are controlled less by toleration than by the moral principles they select. These principles determine what is to be tolerated, not-tolerated, or accepted. Had they selected a different set of principles, different recommendations would likely have been forthcoming. Even some of the observations we made in our brief historical sketch support the suggestion that toleration can at least be somewhat uninteresting, even if it is important. The arguments for and against toleration presented in that chapter have not varied significantly throughout Western European history. The topics themselves changed so that first religious, then political, and finally a wide range of social behavior was brought into the circle of things that are tolerated. But no matter what the topic, the arguments nearly always seemed to be concerned with questions relating to spheres of responsibility, conscience, and especially pragmatic matters. Arguments for and against toleration seemed to be repetitiously uninteresting.

It would appear that the answer to the questions we posed initially in this study—about how important and interesting the toleration concepts are—is "not very." At least a case can be made for such an answer. We, however, wish to draw the opposite conclusion. We do not wish to overrate this concept, but we do wish to clinch the case we have been making all along that the general neglect from which toleration suffers is unfortunate.

The Unique Character of the Toleration Concepts

We have noted that the toleration concepts perform different linguistic functions than such concepts as good-bad and right-wrong. At first glance it seemed that they do not, inasmuch as the moral principles to which we often appeal can apparently be formulated in terms of any of these concepts without a change in meaning. Consider a version of what might be called the noncoercion principle.

A. To the extent that a relationship is coercive, it is not to be tolerated.

152

And now consider the following variants.

    B. To the extent that a relationship is coercive, it is:

1. bad	4. unethical
2. not good	5. wrong
3. immoral	6. not right.

But the meaning of the A-version of this principle is not even close to the meaning of any of the B-versions, appearances to the contrary. For our purposes, the important difference between them is that A directly recommends a *response* to a situation, while the B-versions do not. It is true that in recommending a not-tolerant response one is not really saying anything very specific. This recommendation does not tell us whether the response should be intolerant, where coercion may be employed, or nontolerant, where withdrawal is in order. Even if the proper response were intoleration, rather than nontoleration, the recommendation would still not be very specific, for an intolerant response can take many forms. This nonspecific character of recommendations supporting one or the other of the family of toleration concepts is because, as was shown in chapter 7, all the toleration concepts suffer from response complexity. Nonetheless, though it lacks specificity, the message of the expression "is not to be tolerated" is that the behavior in question must be stopped somehow. The B-versions of the noncoercion principle are not obvious pleas for a response or for action in the way the A-version is. Linguistically they are more like judgments. They do not call for a specific response, though a plea for a response might be derived from them with the addition of other premises.

A closely related, and more important, difference between the toleration concepts and such concepts as good-bad, right-wrong, and ethical-unethical is that the former are trichotomous while the latter pairings are dichotomous only. While the good-bad group of concepts divides the normative realm only into the positive and the negative, the toleration concepts allow for three sorts of response by introducing the possibility of indifference. Thus if indifference is taken into account, good-bad becomes good-indifferent-bad, while the toleration concepts become not-tolerant-tolerant-indifferent-acceptance.

Either way, the toleration concepts add refinement to our normative thinking by providing us with an additional option. Moreover, not-toleration divides into intoleration and nontoleration (in the sense of withdrawal) and thus adds further refinement. Refinement of a similar form is also present on the positive side with such concepts as mere acceptance, acceptance in the community, and approval. Of course, some of the dichotomous concepts are also subject to refinement because built into the logic of the good-bad concepts we have, on the positive side, not only 'good' but 'better' and 'best'. Similar refinement is present on the negative side. Refinement of this sort has not thus far been a topic of our study. However, the toleration concepts can also be characterized in the way good-bad can be through the use of modifying expressions such as "more" and "most." We can, for example, speak of someone as intolerant, very intolerant, and most intolerant. Such refinement is a matter of degree for the most part. Being just that, it leaves the good-bad concepts dichotomous in nature.

Yet in addition to being refinable by degree, the toleration concepts break into qualitatively distinct response types. They tell us, when used prescriptively, that we may respond in one of three qualitatively distinct ways to whatever situations we are facing. So, as we have been arguing throughout this study, the toleration concepts are different from the more commonly discussed normative (including moral) ones in at least two fundamental ways. They are different not only because they are trichotomous in nature but also because they are explicit response concepts. They remind us that we can respond to a situation in three distinct ways.

Ties to Liberal Ideology

Part of our case for saying that the toleration concepts are not uninteresting and unimportant, then, rests upon the specific logical roles they play in normative settings. However, as further support for what we said in chapter 8, we wish now to contend that the toleration concepts are interesting and important because they are essential to the kinds of freedoms basic to a liberal society and thus are essential to the liberal ideology.

To begin to see why they are essential to liberalism, it is useful to imagine a nonliberal society that allows its citizens to act freely only when they exhibit behavior to which it is indifferent or to which it responds with acceptance. A little reflection will show that, with these restrictions, this society would probably forbid certain freedoms, such as speech, and would put limits on many others. In our imaginary society, there might be total or near total freedom to choose what people eat, how they decorate the interior of their homes, the sports they choose to pursue and/or follow as spectators, provided we assume the society is indifferent to such matters. On the more positive side of acceptance, these people might be free to join the army, navy, or air force—all of which would be considered honorable institutions in this society—or possibly work at home as civilians. There might also be somewhat more limited freedoms, delineated by social indifference, possibly encompassing freedom of movement, choice of a job, and the like. Here our imaginary society would restrict people only during such emergencies as war or civil unrest. Inasmuch as most kinds of ordinary day-to-day movement, and their consequences, would be viewed either with approval or

155

with indifference, people would probably be allowed to go where and when they please—up to a point.

But more than a minimal freedom of speech could not be allowed simply because people would, sooner or later, say things of which their society disapproves. Nor would extensive freedom of religion be allowed because, if it were, offensive things would eventually be said and done by those exercising this freedom. Thus, if a second, more liberal society actually *wanted* to allow these freedoms in more than a minimal fashion and if it realized, as it would, that doing so would lead to things being said and done that it could not approve (or view with indifference), that society would have to invent something akin to the concept of toleration to help it achieve its desires. This is not a point of logic because it is theoretically possible that when people exercise their freedom of speech, or other such freedoms, they would never offend or upset others. It is possible that no tolerating would occur in this second society. In the real world, however, the situation would more than likely be otherwise, with the result that these people would have to tolerate a good deal of obnoxious talk and action in order to preserve their liberal freedoms.

Even so, it could be argued that toleration is not particularly important because it represents an ideal or standard for only one of several major normative political stances. Further, as we have argued, it is the various freedoms that make toleration important, not the other way around. Granting this parasitic nature of toleration, the importance of toleration cannot be denied, for without it these freedoms would not exist. If people were given freedom of speech, religion, and the other liberal freedoms only to the extent that other people found these freedoms acceptable (i.e., not merely tolerable), the facts of life suggest that much less freedom would exist in the world than we find even today.

Nor could many so-called personal freedoms exist. These

include not only sexual freedoms but almost all other freedoms having to do with people getting along with one another on a one-to-one basis. Again, the concept of toleration is necessary when, in this less-than-perfect world, we grant each other freedom to do a variety of things that we do not approve. Toleration, then, is needed not only by advocates of a liberal/pluralistic ideology but much more broadly by all those who wish to grant to others a variety of personal freedoms. Yet in granting these freedoms, we contend, one cannot help but adopt a tolerating response. To the extent that these responses make freedom possible, toleration can be thought of as a freedom extender—extending freedom beyond the realm of behavior that is either indifferent or acceptable to us.

As a freedom extender, it might plausibly be supposed that of all the major concepts in the toleration family, toleration itself, as against nontoleration, intoleration, and acceptance, is the head. Indeed we think that this supposition is correct and wish to support it with the following argument. If the concept of toleration were not present in our language, a concept somewhat like *in*toleration would be there in any case. It would not be labeled intoleration, but it would be there in some other guise serving roughly in the capacity of saying "no." We have already remarked that much of our prescriptive language is dichotomous in structure in the sense that the meaning of many prescriptive concepts simply breaks down into "yes" and "no." So if the family of toleration concepts were not in our language, intoleration's function on the extreme negative side, and for that matter acceptance's function on the positive side, would be taken over by one or more of the dichotomous concepts.

But no dichotomous concept could replace toleration, for its function is to interpose itself as a unique response concept between "yes" and "no." Toleration is not "yes" *or* "no," but "yes" *and* "no." It says "Yes, go ahead and do it," but "No, do not expect a smile if you do." It is toleration, not intoleration, nontoleration, acceptance, or even all of the toleration concepts taken together, that creates the trichotomy we have been discussing. It is toleration, therefore, that offers us the possibility of responding to a difficult situation with a degree of flexibility not possible with the dichotomous concepts.

Partisan Nature of the Toleration Concepts

It is response alternatives like toleration that the radicals on the political Left and Right, who respond in right-wrong terms, would foreclose from us. Some would do so because their rigid personalities or their lack of logical acuity does not allow them to think in other than dichotomous terms. Others, like Marcuse, can and do think seriously about toleration but explicitly reject it as an option. With whichever types of intolerant people (and/or society) we are dealing, their responses to difficult situations will differ sharply from the styles of those who tend to respond tolerantly. The responses will differ so sharply that those who are intolerant will tend to look upon the tolerantly responding individuals with disdain. They will look upon these individuals as compromisers at best and as appeasers at worst. They will see them, further, as naive, because tolerant people will optimistically believe that they can stand and move about on the proverbial slippery slope when dealing with important and difficult issues without sliding down to the bottom. Holding the high ground instead, the intolerant people will look down upon the tolerant ones as being excessively flexible and, in this sense, unprincipled.

Actually, we have already dealt with charges like these by, among other things, pointing out that intolerant people are themselves vulnerable to the countercharge of responding in an overly rigid manner. Neither those who are tolerant nor those who are intolerant are totally immune from the fault of excess. Still, the charge that tolerant people are unprincipled needs to be looked at once again so as to put it to rest once and for all.

No doubt, the excesses of the tolerant are many. These people can gradually come to tolerate more things than they should because they are lazy, indecisive, and fuzzy-headed and therefore do not know where to draw the line. Their excesses may even include ignorance, because they may not realize they are tolerating and possibly even slipping ever so slowly into acceptance. However, excesses of one form or another can hardly be attributable only to those who tolerate. As a case in point, tolerant people do not have a monopoly on ignorance. Those who are intolerant also seem to be well endowed. Rather than ignorance, being unprincipled would seem the more likely candidate as the special weakness of those who are tolerant.

In this connection, recall that we observed on several occasions that toleration need not be temporary shelter either for those who are on their way to acceptance or on their way to intoleration (nontoleration). Rather, we said that toleration can be a deliberate and permanent response to a situation or problem (e.g., as it might be if the Decibelians were granted a right to practice their noisy religion). If toleration can result from deliberate choice, toleration hardly sounds like a concept for the fuzzy-headed or the spineless, especially inasmuch as those who must hold their ground as tolerators are likely to be forced to fend off criticism from both sides. If tolerators most often struggle to remain tolerant and do so from conviction, the criticism from those holding the high ground of intoleration should not be that tolerant people are without principle. Instead, if this is a criticism, it should be that tolerant people have principles but that these principles are very difficult to defend.

We can arrive at much the same conclusion by comparing

159

the concept of toleration with that of compromise. Like toleration, compromise is a response concept. To tolerate or to compromise is to respond to an unhappy situation. However, one difference is that compromise is a bilateral response concept requiring adjustments on the part of both sides while toleration is unilateral. While a case can be made for saying that those who compromise are unprincipled in the sense that they cannot help but depart from whatever principles they are holding in order to effect a compromise, those who tolerate need not depart from their principles in the same way. Of course, in a trivial sense, both groups can claim to be principled because each group may be following a general injunction about when to compromise or when to tolerate. With those compromising, the general rule might run: "Compromise, unless you hold all of the cards." A similar rule might be expressed by those tolerating by deleting "compromise" and replacing it with "tolerate." But like those compromising, those tolerating need not follow rules that suggest they are responding from a position of weakness because tolerating can be, and sometimes is, a response from a position of strength. The possibility of tolerating from strength is part of what is meant by saying that it is a freedom extender. It is not as if we tolerate freedom of speech only because we cannot shut people up. In fact, when we are tolerating, we sometimes do not want to be seen as negotiating away bits and pieces of anyone's freedom. Instead, we may want to be seen as voluntarily tolerating in spite of our misgivings.

Recall, for the last time, that toleration is not the ideal-state concept talked of confusedly by Marcuse and others but a concept of the real world where things are less than perfect. Thus, if it means anything, the expression "true toleration" probably has little or nothing to do with acceptance, a concept especially at home in a utopian setting. It has more to do, instead, with our willingness to extend someone some freedom despite our discomfort. This kind of toleration might be called true toleration because its virtue is that it is willingly granted to another person or group against the pressure of our misgivings, and, in this sense, it is born out of struggle. It seems grossly inappropriate to think of those people practicing this kind of toleration as unprincipled.

In addition to being a key normative concept because of its trichotomous characteristics and because it plays a necessary role in liberal ideology as a freedom extender, toleration is a concept within that ideology that presents us with an ideal. However, to say that toleration is a liberal ideal is not to say that cases of tolerating on the political, social, and personal levels are not often triggered by less than idealistic or principled motives. Most people may very well be tolerant for less than ideal reasons, such as laziness, inertia, cowardice, or just plain calculated selfishness. Still, so long as some people can tolerate on principle, in the sense of tolerating for certain normative reasons, that concept assumes importance. It does so not just as a logically necessary aspect of the liberal's ideology but as an aspect that helps to portray what the ideal of the liberal person and the liberal society is about.

Notes

Chapter 1

1. The most common kind of confusion regarding the distinction among the concepts of tolerating, tolerance, and intolerance is to assume that the only options we have are those of intolerance and tolerance. For instance, R. M. Hare in *Freedom and Reason* (New York: Oxford University Press, 1965), pp. 49–50, seems to think that if we are not intolerant, we must be tolerant. But as we shall see later, not-tolerating is not the same as intolerance; so this is an option. Ignoring is not the same as tolerating, so this is another possibility. Or, we might decide to accept something, and that represents still another option. Lord Devlin makes the complementary mistake of assuming that if a practice should not be tolerated, then our only option is to be intolerant of it (Patrick Devlin, "Morals and the Criminal Law" in *The Enforcement of Morals* [London: Oxford University Press, 1965], pp. 1–25).

Similarly, Mill is guilty of failing to realize that the options of tolerating and accepting differ. In *On Liberty* he mixes arguments on behalf of the position that we ought to tolerate certain kinds of actions (based on the self-regarding/other-regarding distinction) with arguments that voicing views we find distasteful may be useful in achieving truth and in extending the range of liberty. The first arguments are directed at that which we should tolerate—without attempting to change our attitudes—while the second group of arguments is directed at our attitudes, in the attempt to change them from disapproval to acceptance. See John Stuart Mill, *On Liberty*, ed. Alburey Castell (New York: Appleton-Century-Crofts, 1947), pp. 10, 16.

2. Lord Devlin and James Fitzjames Stephen, Mill's critic, do not

recognize this disjunction. They presume that once we have deter-mined that something is wrong or immoral, we then have the obliga-tion to root it out. See Devlin, "Morals and the Criminal Law," pp. 24–25, and James Fitzjames Stephen, *Liberty, Equality, Fraternity* (London: Smith, Elder, 1873), pp. 84–85.

This distinction is recognized and understood by Etienne Gilson, who says: "Tolerance does not consist in accepting all philosophical statements as more or less probable, but, being absolutely certain that one of them is true and the other false, in letting everyone be free to speak his own mind," in *Dogmatism & Tolerance* (New Brunswick, N.J.: Rutgers University Press, 1952), pp. 7–8. Another who recognizes this distinction is Jay Newman, in "The Idea of Reli-gious Tolerance," *American Philosophical Quarterly* 15 (July 1978): 187–88.

3. See, for example, Geoffrey Harrison, "Relativism and Toler-ance," *Ethics* 86 (January 1976): 127.

4. This point is recognized by Maurice Cranston in his useful ar-ticle "Toleration," in *The Encyclopedia of Philosophy*, ed. Paul Edwards, 8 vols. (New York: Macmillan, 1967), 8:143–46.

5. Once more R. M. Hare appears not to recognize this distinction when he states: "He [the liberal] may even think that a diversity of ideals is in itself a good thing. . . . If the liberal's ideal is any of these kinds, he is not betraying it but following it if he tolerates the other peoples' pursuit of their ideals" (*Freedom and Reason*, p. 180). The only exception Hare allows here is when he discusses the case in which the pursuit by one person of one set of ideals interferes with the pursuit by another of a differing set of ideals (p. 179). Our posi-tive attitude does not settle the issue in this case, however, for we may have a variety of reasons for failing to tolerate that which we respect—as the example in the text shows.

6. One scholar, Charles W. Hendel, Jr., has noted: "His own ge-nius consisted, then, in a remarkable power of appreciating the dif-ferent convictions at stake, and at the same time of seeing all the logical difficulties in the several arguments. . . . Though always very much disposed to believe with the 'common people,' as he himself

said, he could not . . . ignore his doubts. It was necessary for him, therefore, to think this matter out for himself" (Charles W. Hendel, Jr., ed., *Hume Selections* [New York: Charles Scribner's Sons, 1927], pp. 6–7).

7. Thomas K. Hearn, Jr., develops the view that tolerance is open-mindedness in "On Tolerance," *Southern Journal of Philosophy* (Summer and Fall 1970): 223–32.

8. Mill, *On Liberty,* p. 56.

Chapter 2

1. John Searle, *Speech Acts* (Cambridge: Cambridge University Press, 1969), p. 16: "The unit of linguistic communication is not, as has generally been supposed, the symbol, word, or sentence, or even the token of the symbol, word, or sentence, but rather the production or issuance of the symbol or word or sentence in the performance of the speech act. To take the token as a message is to take it as a produced or issued token. More precisely, the production or issuance of a sentence token under certain conditions is a speech act, and speech acts (of certain kinds to be explained later) are the basic or minimal units of linguistic communication."

2. Nick Fotion, "Speech Activity and Language Use," *Philosophia* 8 (October 1979): 615–38.

3. John Searle, "A Taxonomy of Illocutionary Acts," in *Expression and Meaning* (Cambridge: Cambridge University Press, 1979), pp. 1–29. Searle identifies five major types of illocutionary (speech) acts. The point of directives is "that they are attempts (of varying degrees, and hence, more precisely, they are determinates of the determinable which includes attempting) by the speaker to get the hearer to do something" (p. 10).

4. Marcuse implies as much when he talks of "repressive tolerance," "destructive tolerance," and "indiscriminate tolerance." Presumably these undesirable forms of tolerance are matched by more desirable forms. More explicitly, tolerance is seen as a positive state for him when he says "the telos of tolerance is truth" and "Liberating

tolerance, then, would mean intolerance against movements from the Right, and toleration of movements from the Left" (Herbert Marcuse, "Repressive Tolerance," in Robert Paul Wolff, Barrington Moore, Jr., and Herbert Marcuse, *A Critique of Pure Tolerance* [Boston: Beacon Press, 1969], pp. 90, 109).

Chapter 3

1. We wish to thank an astute reader for bringing this important example to our attention.

Chapter 4

1. The views expressed here are similar to those that support what Hart calls the minimum content of law (H. L. A. Hart, *The Concept of Law* [Oxford: Oxford University Press, 1961], pp. 189–95).

2. In the strict sense of the word, children cannot be treated paternalistically. Only adults can be treated in a way *similar* to the way parents treat their children. See Nick Fotion "Paternalism," *Ethics* 89 (January 1979): 191–98.

Chapter 6

1. Joseph Lecler, *Toleration and the Reformation*, trans. T. L. Westow, 2 vols. (New York: Association Press, 1960), 1:20.

2. L. R. Farnell, *The Higher Aspects of Greek Religion* (London: Williams and Norgate, 1912), pp. 65, 73–74. For a similar point see Thaddeus Zielinski, *The Religion of Ancient Greece*, trans. George Rapall Noyes (Freeport, N.Y.: Books for Libraries Press, 1971), p. 107.

3. See Lecler, *Toleration and the Reformation*, 1:21, and Hendrik Van Loon, *Tolerance* (Boni and Liversight, 1925), pp. 56–58, as well as John Ferguson, *The Religions of the Roman Empire* (Ithaca, N.Y.: Cornell University Press, 1970), pp. 233–35.

4. Matt. 22:21.

5. Lecler, *Toleration and the Reformation*, 1:149–55. For an account of the vicissitudes of this sort of argument see J. W. Allen, *En-

NOTES TO CHAPTER 6

glish Political Thought 1603–1644 (Hamden, Conn.: Archon, 1967), p. 211.

6. See Van Loon, *Tolerance,* pp. 34, 68; Martin P. Nilsson, *A History of Greek Religion,* trans. F. J. Fielden (Oxford: Clarendon Press, 1949), pp. 251–52; and R. M. Ogilvie, *The Romans and Their Gods* (London: Chatto and Windus, 1969), pp. 2–3.

7. This idea is developed and elaborated in H. F. Russell-Smith, *The Theory of Religious Liberty* (Cambridge: Cambridge University Press, 1911).

8. Ibid., pp. 1–2.

9. John Locke, *A Letter Concerning Toleration,* ed. Mario Montuori (The Hague: Martinus Nijhoff, 1963) and Russell-Smith, *Theory of Religious Liberty,* p. 106.

10. Locke, *Letter Concerning Toleration,* pp. 43, 79–80, 101.

11. John Stuart Mill, *On Liberty,* ed. Alburey Castell (New York: Appleton-Century-Crofts, 1947), p. 32.

12. Ibid., p. 56.

13. Ibid., p. 67.

14. Samples of Devlin's and Hart's positions on this issue, along with discussions of their views by other scholars, have been usefully collected by Richard A. Wasserstrom in *Morality and the Law* (Belmont, Calif.: Wadsworth, 1971).

15. Useful works dealing with the topic of civil disobedience include James F. Childress, *Civil Disobedience and Political Obligation* (New Haven: Yale University Press, 1971); Carl Cohen, *Civil Disobedience* (New York: Columbia University Press, 1971); Peter Singer, *Democracy and Disobedience* (Oxford: Clarendon Press, 1973); Michael Walzer, *Obligations* (Cambridge: Harvard University Press, 1970); J. Roland Pennock and John W. Chapman, eds., *Political and Legal Obligation* (New York: Atherton Press, 1970).

16. Mill himself argued that self-regarding acts should be tolerated but acts that affect others need not be. In contemporary discussions, however, a broader view is taken. It is argued that actions that affect

NOTES TO CHAPTER 6

others in important ways should often be tolerated. See Mill, *On Liberty*, pp. 55–56. A good example of a contemporary view of these matters is Ronald Dworkin, "On Not Prosecuting Civil Disobedience," *New York Review of Books*, June 6, 1968, reprinted in Joel Feinberg and Hyman Gross, eds., *Philosophy of Law*, 2d ed. (Belmont, Calif.: Wadsworth, 1980), pp. 125–34.

17. Robert Nozick, *Anarchy, State and Utopia* (New York: Basic Books, 1974). Nozick has received more attention than other contemporary proponents of radical individualism. Others who would subscribe to views roughly similar to those of Nozick include: Milton Friedman, *Capitalism and Freedom* (Chicago: University of Chicago Press, 1962); Ayn Rand, *The Virtue of Selfishness* (New York: New American Library, 1965); and Murray Rothbard, *For a New Liberty* (New York: Macmillan, 1973).

18. Nozick, *Anarchy, State and Utopia*, pp. 57–58, and Frederick A. Hayek, *The Road to Serfdom* (Chicago: University of Chicago Press, 1944), pp. 58–59. This idea is, of course, suggested by the self-regarding/other-regarding distinction devised by Mill, *On Liberty*, p. 10.

19. See, for example, Nozick, *Anarchy, State and Utopia*, p. 58.

20. Such actions include, it should be noted, those intended to assist or benefit the affected party as well as those that harm him or her. Any action that affects the particular individual without that person's consent is illegitimate in this view. Recall that "paternalism" became a pejorative term only with the rise of liberalism. See Nozick, ibid.

21. See, for example, Hayek, *Road to Serfdom*, pp. 57–58, as well as Mill, *On Liberty*, p. 12.

22. Perhaps the most striking exemplar of this facet of radical individualism is Rand, *Virtue of Selfishness*, pp. vii–x, 13–35.

23. Mill, *On Liberty*, pp. 10–11.

24. Ibid., pp. 76–77, 84.

25. As examples of the collectivist outlook, we will mention the views of the classical Greeks, Hegel, Marx, and the Roman Catholic

church. All these disparate perspectives espouse the three core ideas of collectivism. We do not mean to imply that the ideologies embodied in these examples are equivalent in all aspects, or even most, but merely that they agree in holding to the main tenets of collectivism. For the idea of society being an organic whole, see: George H. Sabine, A History of Political Theory, 3d ed. (New York: Holt, Rinehart and Winston, 1961), pp. 12–13, for clarification of the Greek view; T. M. Knox, trans., Hegel's Philosophy of Right (Oxford: Clarendon Press, 1942), pp. 155–56, 164–79, as well as Gustav Emil Mueller, trans., Hegel's Encyclopedia of Philosophy (New York: Philosophical Library, 1959), pp. 245–46, for Hegel's view; and T. B. Bottomore, trans. and ed., Karl Marx: Selected Writings in Sociology & Social Philosophy (New York: McGraw-Hill, 1964), p. 77; and for the Roman Catholic view see Karl Adam, The Spirit of Catholicism, trans. Justin McCann (Garden City, N.Y.: Doubleday, 1954), pp. 36–37.

26. "The World of Islam," pp. 40–49, and "A Faith of Law and Submission," pp. 50–52, Time (April 16, 1979).

27. Harold J. Berman, Justice in the U.S.S.R., rev. ed. (New York: Vintage Books, 1963).

28. Sabine, History of Political Theory, p. 12, outlines the Greek view on this matter. For Hegel's perspective see Mueller, Hegel's Encyclopedia, pp. 245–46, and Knox, Hegel's Philosophy, pp. 155–56.

29. Lewis S. Feuer, ed., Basic Writings on Politics & Philosophy (by) Karl Marx and Friederich Engels (Garden City, N.Y.: Doubleday, 1959), pp. 258–59.

30. As the commentator Karl Adam says, "the community and not the individual is the bearer of the Spirit of Jesus" (Spirit of Catholicism, p. 38).

31. For example, see Knox, Hegel's Philosophy, pp. 216–20.

32. For an exposition of the Greek view of these matters see Sabine, History of Political Theory, pp. 17–19; for Hegel's view see Mueller, Hegel's Encyclopedia, pp. 245–46, Knox, Hegel's Philosophy, p. 156, and Sabine, ibid., p. 653; for the Marxist view see Bottomore, Karl Marx, pp. 77, 247.

169

33. Sabine, *History of Political Theory*, pp. 16–17, for the Greek outlook; Mueller, *Hegel's Encyclopedia*, pp. 246–47, for Hegel's view; and for the Marxist view see Bottomore, *Karl Marx*, pp. 222–23, 234–37, 256–58.

34. See, for example, Ellsworth Raymond, *The Soviet State*, 2d ed. (New York: New York University Press, 1978), pp. 273–91; and O. Edmund Clubb, *20th Century China*, 2d ed. (New York: Columbia University Press, 1972), pp. 311–12, 457–64.

35. This idea is mentioned by Robert Paul Wolff, "Beyond Tolerance," in Robert Paul Wolff, Barrington Moore, Jr., and Herbert Marcuse, *A Critique of Pure Tolerance* (Boston: Beacon Press, 1969), pp. 36–37, and in the article "Pluralism" in Edwin A. Seligman, ed., *Encyclopaedia of the Social Sciences*, 15 vols. (New York: Macmillan, 1934), 12:173. Some of the major works of the pluralist tradition include: Harold J. Laski, *A Grammar of Politics*, 4th ed. (New Haven: Yale University Press, 1939); A. D. Lindsay, *The Modern Democratic State* (New York: Oxford University Press, 1943); Mary Parker Follett, *The New State* (New York: Longmans, 1918); R. A. Dahl, *A Preface to Democratic Theory* (Chicago: University of Chicago Press, 1956); and William Kornhauser, *The Politics of Mass Society* (New York: Free Press, 1969).

36. Seligman, *Encyclopaedia*, 12: 171; Grant McConnell, "The Public Virtues of Private Association," in J. Roland Pennock and John W. Chapman, eds., *Voluntary Associations: Nomos XI* (New York: Atherton Press, 1969), pp. 149–52; Wolff et al., *Critique*, pp. 6–8; and William E. Connolly, "The Challenge to Pluralist Theory," in *The Bias of Pluralism*, ed. William E. Connolly (New York: Atherton Press, 1969), pp. 3–8.

37. Seligman, *Encyclopaedia*, 12: 171; Laski, *Grammar of Politics*, pp. 17–25; and Wolff et al., *Critique*, pp. 6–7.

38. Connolly, "Challenge to Pluralist Theory," p. 8; David Nicholls, *Three Varieties of Pluralism* (New York: St. Martin's Press, 1974), p. 2; William Alton Kelso, *American Democratic Theory* (Westport, Conn.: Greenwood Press, 1978), p. 9; and Wolff, "Beyond Tolerance," pp. 10–12.

39. McConnell, "Public Virtues of Private Association," pp. 147–50; Connolly, "Challenge to Pluralist Theory," p. 4; Laski, *Grammar of Politics*, pp. 429–32; Nicholls, *Three Varieties of Pluralism*, p. 61; and Wolff, "Beyond Tolerance," p. 16.

40. See, for example, Connolly, "Challenge to Pluralist Theory," p. 17; Wolff et al., *Critique*, pp. 49–51; and McConnell, "Public Virtues of Private Association," pp. 156–57.

41. Wolff, "Beyond Tolerance," pp. 15–17; Kelso, *American Democratic Theory*, pp. 242–47; Connolly, "Challenge to Pluralist Theory," pp. 8–13; and McConnell, "Public Virtues of Private Association," p. 150.

42. John Rawls appears to accept this argument (*A Theory of Justice* [Cambridge: Harvard University Press, 1971], pp. 209–10). He acknowledges that his argument is inspired by Mill's *On Liberty*. Jay Newman makes a similar argument in "The Idea of Religious Tolerance," *American Philosophical Quarterly* 15 (July 1978): 190.

43. This argument, taken from Thoreau, is noted by Singer, *Democracy and Disobedience*, p. 94. The supremacy of conscience is noted in Roman Catholic doctrine, as well. See Adam, *Spirit of Catholicism*, p. 207.

44. This point is mentioned by Alan Donagan, *The Theory of Morality* (Chicago: University of Chicago Press, 1977), p. 135; Stephen David Ross, *The Nature of Moral Responsibility* (Detroit: Wayne State University Press, 1973), p. 185; and Lecler, *Toleration and the Reformation*, p. 94.

45. Donagan, *Theory of Morality*, pp. 135–36.

46. James F. Childress argues this point in "Appeals to Conscience," *Ethics* 89 (July 1979): 318, 330–31.

47. For a contemporary discussion of this issue see Newman, "Idea of Religious Tolerance," pp. 190–91. Also see David G. Ritchie, *Natural Rights* (1894; reprint, George Allen and Unwin, 1952), p. 168.

48. This point is made by Adam, *Spirit of Catholicism*, pp. 206–12.

49. John Locke offered this argument to show that Muslims should not be tolerated. See Locke, *Letter Concerning Toleration*, pp. 91–92. Note also Russell-Smith, *Theory of Religious Liberty*, p. 119.

50. This point is noted in Maurice Cranston "Toleration," in *The Encyclopedia of Philosophy*, ed. Paul Edwards, 8 vols. (New York: Macmillan, 1967), 8:146.

51. A. Lubow and others, "Homosexual Teacher," *Newsweek* (December 18, 1978): 91.

52. Lecler, *Toleration and the Reformation*, pp. 24, 71, 86–87.

53. K. M. Chrysler, "Marcos Tells Why He Chose Martial Law," *U.S. News* (October 16, 1972): 36–38.

54. E. M. Reingold and S. Chang, "Chun: A Shadowy Strongman," *Time* (May 26, 1980): 32.

55. This facet of Burke's thought is emphasized by Sabine, *History of Political Theory*, pp. 607–10.

56. "Nicaragua: Life in the Bunker Republic," *Time* (December 14, 1981): 48–49, gives an example of this kind of argument offered by the representatives of the Sandinista government at the time when they still retained power in Nicaragua.

57. This argument was prominent in seventeenth-century England, as noted by Allen, *English Political Thought*, pp. 2–6.

58. This argument cuts both ways. Some have argued that tolerance of various religious groups is necessary to preserve good civil order, as noted in Russell-Smith, *Theory of Religious Liberty*, p. 55, while Allen (*English Political Thought*, p. 206) notes that in the past there has been some uncertainty as to whether suppression of dissidents will foster or undermine social order.

59. The most vigorous proponent of this view in recent times is, of course, Patrick Devlin. His argument is worked out in the article "Morals and the Criminal Law," collected in his work *Enforcement of Morals*, pp. 1–25.

60. James Fitzjames Stephen, *Liberty, Equality, Fraternity* (London: Smith, Elder, 1873), pp. 136–46, and Devlin, *Enforcement of Morals*, pp. 8–11.

61. "Icelanders Only Want to Be Left Alone," *New York Times*, December 15, 1979, p. 3.

62. B. Krisher, "Japan: Boat People Stay Away," *Newsweek* (September 3, 1979): 46; R. Carroll and others, "The Debris of Our War," *Newsweek* (April 17, 1978): 70–73; and H. Grunwald, "Arguing with South Africa," *Time* (June 27, 1977): 32.

63. Ritchie mentions this argument (*Natural Rights*, pp. 169–73), and it is accepted by Stephen (*Liberty, Equality, Fraternity*, p. 87).

64. This point is noted by Karel Hulicka and Irene M. Hulicka, *Soviet Institutions, the Individual and Society* (Boston: Christopher, 1967), pp. 581–84.

65. Mill, *On Liberty*, pp. 46, 67, 72.

66. Ibid., p. 51.

67. Jean Bodin, *Colloquium of the Seven about the Secrets of the Sublime*, trans. Marion Daniels Kuntz (Princeton: Princeton University Press, 1975), pp. xli–xlii.

68. Russell-Smith, *Theory of Religious Liberty*, pp. 62–63.

Chapter 7

1. Thomas C. Wilson, "Urbanism and Tolerance: A Test of Some Hypotheses Drawn from Wirth and Stouffer," *American Sociological Review* 50 (February 1985): 117–23. Wilson's results are consistent with earlier sociological studies in suggesting "that urbanism *per se* increases tolerance for a variety of groups whose members hold unpopular attitudes if not ideas and interests" (p. 117). These so-called target groups include atheists, racists, homosexuals, communists, and militarists. He further argues that "urbanism appears to increase tolerance for all target groups, apparently without regard to the content of group members' ideas, attitudes, and the like" (p. 122).

Claude S. Fischer (*To Dwell Among Friends: Personal Networks in Town and City* [Chicago: University of Chicago Press, 1982], p. 74) concurs. Interestingly enough, Fischer also suggests that what we have been calling nontoleration increases in urban centers because ethnic, religious, sexual, and other subgroups tend to escape into the city. In the larger cities especially, they gain an identity after the subgroups grow enough to reach a critical mass. No doubt other variables affect the level of toleration practiced in a community. Allan L. McCutcheon ("A Latent Class Analysis of Tolerance for Nonconformity in the American Public," *Public Opinion Quarterly* 49 [Winter 1985]: 474–88) argues for a correlation between increased tolerance and increased education. He also argues that younger people tend to be more tolerant than older ones. John L. Sullivan, James Piereson, and George E. Marcus (*Political Tolerance and American Democracy* [Chicago: University of Chicago Press, 1982]) argue for the importance of a sense of increased security and increased level of tolerance (chap. 8).

2. It should be noted that many of the examples of uses cited in chapters 2, 3, and 4 substantiate this point. Most of them represent "reflective" uses where speakers are talking about their tolerating in retrospect rather than in the actual tolerating situation. The exceptional cases include those discussed in chapter 2 where the speakers warn those who are being tolerated that they are near the border of toleration/intoleration. In view of the point that the toleration concept and its surrogates are often not used at all, even though much tolerating is going on, it should also be noted that many of the uses cited in the early chapters have a certain air of artificiality to them. It was necessary to cite these uses (even if many of them are rarer than it might at first appear) just to get the discussion under way.

3. See Wasserstrom's "Is Adultery Immoral?" in *Today's Moral Problems*, ed. Richard A. Wasserstrom, 2d ed. (New York: Macmillan, 1979), pp. 288–300. He uses a variation of the Purification Strategy throughout this article. Lars O. Ericsson ("Charges Against Prostitution: An Attempt at a Philosophical Assessment," *Ethics* 90 [April 1980]: 335–66) develops a similar argument.

Chapter 8

1. *A Critique of Pure Tolerance* (Boston: Beacon Press, 1969) with essays by Robert Paul Wolff, Barrington Moore, Jr., and Herbert Marcuse is representative. The three contributors, writing from the perspective of the political Left, view their project as a critical response to liberal democracy. Wolff's essay is also included in his extended response to liberalism, *The Poverty of Liberalism* (Boston: Beacon Press, 1968).

2. A cursory reading of Alburey Castell's edition of Mill's *On Liberty* (New York: Appleton-Century-Crofts, 1947) yielded a mention in passing of toleration and intoleration on pp. 8 and 47; of religious toleration on pp. 14, 27, and 93; of the Roman Catholic church as "the most intolerant of churches" on p. 20; of toleration on pp. 28, 31n, 51, 68, 86n, and 100; social intolerance on p. 32; of intolerance on pp. 30, 54, 69, and 73; and, finally, of moral intolerance on p. 84. This listing is no doubt incomplete, but it is important to notice that toleration and its variants are neither analyzed nor applied in any systematic fashion. They are only mentioned.

3. John Rawls, *A Theory of Justice* (Cambridge: Harvard University Press, 1971), pp. 211–21.

4. See, for example, Mill's earliest critic James Fitzjames Stephen, *Liberty, Equality, Fraternity* (London: Smith, Elder, 1873); Wolff, *Poverty of Liberalism*; or Joel Feinberg, *Social Philosophy* (Englewood Cliffs, N.J.: Prentice-Hall, 1973).

5. See Feinberg, *Social Philosophy*, pp. 20–54. A useful recent example of the legal application of the principle of privacy can be found in Justice William Brennan's dissent in *Hardwick* v. *Georgia*, a hotly contested Supreme Court case dealing with laws governing sexual conduct. At the time it was clearly recognized that the principle of privacy was connected with the issue. See "Excerpts from the Court Opinions on Homosexual Relations," *New York Times*, July 1, 1986, p. A18.

6. Rawls, *Theory of Justice*, pp. 195–221.

7. Feinberg, *Social Philosophy*, pp. 20–54.

8. Ronald Dworkin, *Taking Rights Seriously* (Cambridge: Harvard University Press, 1977), pp. 223–39. Mill also wrestles with this difficulty (*On Liberty*, pp. 75–82).

9. Mill, *On Liberty*, pp. 10–11.

10. Ibid., pp. 53–54.

11. Wolff, *Poverty of Liberalism*, p. 18.

12. Rawls, *Theory of Justice*, pp. 142–61; and Alan Gewirth, *Reason and Morality* (Chicago: University of Chicago Press, 1978), pp. 129–98.

13. Mill, *On Liberty*, pp. 4–10.

14. Wolff, *Poverty of Liberalism*, p. 18.

15. Mill, *On Liberty*, pp. 55–74.

16. See, for example, Furukawa Tesshi, "The Individual in Japanese Ethics," pp. 228–44; Kosaka Masaaki, "The Status and the Role of the Individual in Japanese Society," pp. 245–61; and Kawashima Takeyoshi, "The Status of the Individual in the Notion of Law, Right, and Social Order in Japan," pp. 262–87—all in *The Mind of Japan*, ed. Charles A. Moore (Honolulu: University Press of Hawaii, 1967).

Chapter 9

1. Herbert Marcuse, "Repressive Tolerance" and "Postscript 1968," in Robert Paul Wolff, Barrington Moore, Jr., and Herbert Marcuse, *A Critique of Pure Tolerance* (Boston: Beacon Press, 1969), pp. 82–84, 104–05. (Because we will be making numerous references to this work, future citations will be placed in the text enclosed in parentheses.)

2. A liberal argument *in favor of* toleration is based on the claim that it provides a harmless safety valve for dissent. See, for example, David G. Ritchie, *Natural Rights* (1894; reprint, London: George Allen and Unwin, 1952), p. 195. In effect, what Marcuse has done is to claim that the practice of toleration in liberal society functions in

this way—and to claim that it is repressive for this reason. He has taken an old argument supporting toleration and turned it around.

3. It is odd that Marcuse should make this claim about the relation between education and the capacity for objectivity, for few in the cadre of the most highly educated—other college professors like Marcuse himself—agreed with his position.

4. John Stuart Mill, *On Liberty*, ed. Alburey Castell (New York: Appleton-Century-Crofts, 1947), p. 58.

Selected Bibliography

Books

Adam, Karl. *The Spirit of Catholicism*. Translated by Justin McCann. Garden City, N.Y.: Doubleday, 1954.

Allen, J. W. *English Political Thought 1603–1644*. Hamden, Conn.: Archon, 1967.

Aristotle. *Nichomachean Ethics*. In the *Basic Works of Aristotle*, translated by Richard McKeon. New York: Random House, 1941.

Beitz, Charles R. *Political Theory and International Relations*. Princeton: Princeton University Press, 1979.

Berman, Harold J. *Justice in the U.S.S.R.* Rev. ed. New York: Vintage Books, 1963.

Bissell, Richard E., and Chester A. Crocker, eds. *South Africa into the 1980s*. Boulder, Colo.: Westview Press, 1979.

Bodin, Jean. *Colloquium of the Seven about the Secrets of the Sublime*. Translated by Marion Daniels Kuntz. Princeton: Princeton University Press, 1975.

Bottomore, T. B., trans. and ed. *Karl Marx: Selected Writings in Sociology & Social Philosophy*. New York: McGraw-Hill, 1964.

Brandt, Richard B. *A Theory of the Good and the Right*. Oxford: Clarendon Press, 1979.

Cecil, Andrew R. *Equality, Tolerance, and Loyalty*. Austin: University of Texas Press, 1990.

Childress, James F. *Civil Disobedience and Political Obligation*. New Haven: Yale University Press, 1971.

SELECTED BIBLIOGRAPHY

Clubb, O. Edmund. *20th Century China.* 2d ed. New York: Columbia University Press, 1972.

Cohen, Carl. *Civil Disobedience.* New York: Columbia University Press, 1971.

Connolly, William E., ed. *The Bias of Pluralism.* New York: Atherton Press, 1969.

Dahl, R. A. *A Preface to Democratic Theory.* Chicago: University of Chicago Press, 1956.

Devlin, Patrick. *The Enforcement of Morals.* London: Oxford University Press, 1965.

DeVos, George A., ed. *Socialization for Achievement.* Berkeley and Los Angeles: University of California Press, 1973.

Diamond, Cora, and Jenny Teichman. *Intention and Intentionality: Essays in Honor of G. E. M. Anscombe.* Ithaca, N.Y.: Cornell University Press, 1979.

Donagan, Alan. *The Theory of Morality.* Chicago: University of Chicago Press, 1977.

Dworkin, Ronald. *Taking Rights Seriously.* Cambridge: Harvard University Press, 1977.

Edwards, Paul, ed. *The Encyclopedia of Philosophy.* 8 vols. New York: Macmillan, 1967.

Enloc, Cynthia H. *Ethnic Conflicts and Political Development.* Boston: Little, Brown, 1973.

Farnell, L. R. *The Higher Aspects of Greek Religion.* London: Williams and Norgate, 1912.

Feinberg, Joel. *Social Philosophy.* Englewood Cliffs, N.J.: Prentice-Hall, 1973.

Feinberg, Joel, and Hyman Gross, eds. *Philosophy of Law.* 2d ed. Belmont, Calif.: Wadsworth, 1980.

SELECTED BIBLIOGRAPHY

Ferguson, John. *The Religions of the Roman Empire*. Ithaca, N.Y.: Cornell University Press, 1970.

Feuer, Lewis S., ed. *Basic Writings on Politics & Philosophy* (by) Karl Marx and Friedrich Engels. Garden City, N.Y.: Doubleday, 1959.

Fischer, Claude S. *To Dwell Among Friends: Personal Networks in Town and City*. Chicago: University of Chicago Press, 1982.

Follett, Mary Parker. *The New State*. New York: Longmans, 1918.

Frankena, William K., and John T. Granrose, eds. *Introductory Readings in Ethics*. Englewood Cliffs, N.J.: Prentice-Hall, 1974.

French, Peter A., ed. *Conscientious Actions*. Cambridge, Mass.: Shenkman, 1974.

Fried, Charles. *Right and Wrong*. Cambridge: Harvard University Press, 1978.

Friedman, Milton. *Capitalism and Freedom*. Chicago: University of Chicago Press, 1962.

Gelfand, Donald E., and Russell D. Lee, eds. *Ethnic Conflicts and Power: A Cross-National Perspective*. New York: John Wiley and Sons, 1971.

Gert, Bernard. *The Moral Rules*. New York: Harper and Row, 1970.

Gewirth, Alan. *Reason and Morality*. Chicago: University of Chicago Press, 1978.

Gilson, Etienne. *Dogmatism & Tolerance*. New Brunswick, N.J.: Rutgers University Press, 1952.

Glazer, Nathan. *Affirmative Discrimination*. New York: Basic Books, 1975.

Gouinlock, James, ed. *The Moral Writings of John Dewey*. New York: Macmillan, 1976.

Hare, R. M. *Freedom and Reason*. New York: Oxford University Press, 1965.

SELECTED BIBLIOGRAPHY

Hart, H. L. A. *The Concept of Law.* Oxford: Oxford University Press, 1961.

Hayek, Frederick A. *The Road to Serfdom.* Chicago: University of Chicago Press, 1944.

Held, Virginia, Kai Nielsen, and Charles Parsons, eds. *Philosophy & Political Action.* New York: Oxford University Press, 1972.

Hendel, Charles W., Jr., ed. *Hume Selections.* New York: Charles Scribner's Sons, 1927.

Horton, John, and Susan Mendus, eds. *Aspects of Tolerance.* London: Methuen, 1985.

Hulicka, Karel, and Irene M. Hulicka. *Soviet Institutions, the Individual and Society.* Boston: Christopher, 1967.

Hume, David. *A Treatise of Human Nature.* Edited by L. A. Selby-Bigge. Oxford: Clarendon Press, 1951.

Kelso, William Alton. *American Democratic Theory.* Westport, Conn.: Greenwood Press, 1978.

King, Preston T. *Toleration.* New York: St. Martin's Press, 1976.

Knox, T. M., trans. *Hegel's Philosophy of Right.* Oxford: Clarendon Press, 1942.

Kornhauser, William. *The Politics of Mass Society.* New York: Free Press, 1969.

Kurtz, Paul, and Svetozar Stojanovic. *Tolerance and Revolution.* Belgrade, Yugoslavia: Beogradski Graticki Zavod, 1970.

Laski, Harold J. *A Grammar of Politics.* 4th ed. New Haven: Yale University Press, 1939.

Latourette, Kenneth Scott. *The Chinese: Their History and Culture.* 4th ed. New York: Macmillan, 1964.

Lecler, Joseph. *Toleration and the Reformation.* 2 vols. Translated by T. L. Westow. New York: Association Press, 1960.

SELECTED BIBLIOGRAPHY

Lindsay, A. D. *The Modern Democratic State.* New York: Oxford University Press, 1943.

Locke, John. *A Letter Concerning Toleration.* Edited by Mario Montuori. The Hague: Martinus Nijhoff, 1963.

———. *The Second Treatise of Government.* Edited by Thomas P. Peardon. New York: Library of Liberal Arts, 1952.

Long, Thomas. *The Letter for Toleration Decipher'd and the Absurdity and Impiety of an Absolute Toleration Demonstrated by the Judgment of the Presbyterians, Independents, and by Mr. Calvin, Mr. Baxter, and the Parliament, 1662.* London: Freeman Collins, 1689.

Love, Thomas T. *John Courtney Murray: Contemporary Church-State Theory.* Garden City, N.Y.: Doubleday, 1965.

McClosky, Herbert, and Anita Brill. *Dimensions of Tolerance: What Americans Believe about Civil Liberties.* New York: Russell Sage Foundation, 1983.

McMurrin, Sterling M., ed. *The Tanner Lectures on Human Values, 1980.* Vol. 1. Salt Lake City: University of Utah Press, 1980.

Mayo, Bernard. *Ethics and the Moral Life.* London: Macmillan, 1958.

Meiland, Jack, and Michael Krausz, eds. *Relativism: Cognitive and Moral.* Notre Dame: University of Notre Dame Press, 1982.

Mendel, Arthur P., ed. *Essential Works of Marxism.* New York: Bantam Books, 1961.

Mendus, Susan. *Toleration and the Limits of Liberalism.* Atlantic Highlands, N.J.: Humanities Press, 1989.

——— , ed. *Justifying Toleration.* Cambridge: Cambridge University Press, 1988.

Mendus, Susan, and David Edwards, eds. *On Toleration.* Oxford: Clarendon Press, 1987.

SELECTED BIBLIOGRAPHY

Mill, John Stuart. *On Liberty*. Edited by Alburey Castell. New York: Appleton-Century-Crofts, 1947.

Milton, John. *Of True Religion, Haeresie, Schism, Toleration, and What Best Means May be Us'd Against the Growth of Popery*. London, 1673.

Moore, Charles A., ed. *The Mind of Japan*. Honolulu: University Press of Hawaii, 1967.

Mueller, Gustav Emil, trans. *Hegel's Encyclopedia of Philosophy*. New York: Philosophical Library, 1959.

Newman, Jay. *Foundations of Religious Tolerance*. Toronto: University of Toronto Press, 1982.

Nicholls, David. *Three Varieties of Pluralism*. New York: St. Martin's Press, 1974.

Nilsson, Martin P. *A History of Greek Religion*. Translated by F. J. Fielden. Oxford: Clarendon Press, 1949.

Novak, Michael. *The Rise of the Unmeltable Ethnics*. New York: Macmillan, 1971.

Nozick, Robert. *Anarchy, State and Utopia*. New York: Basic Books, 1974.

Ogilvie, R. M. *The Romans and Their Gods*. London: Chatto and Windus, 1969.

Pennock, J. Roland, and John W. Chapman, eds. *Political and Legal Obligation*. New York: Atherton Press, 1970.

———. *Voluntary Associations: Nomos XI*. New York: Atherton Press, 1969.

Plato. *Republic*. Translated by Francis MacDonald Cornford. New York: Oxford University Press, 1975.

Rand, Ayn. *The Virtue of Selfishness*. New York: New American Library, 1965.

184

Rawls, John. *A Theory of Justice.* Cambridge: Harvard University Press, 1971.

Raymond, Ellsworth. *The Soviet State.* 2d ed. New York: New York University Press, 1978.

Richards, David A. J. *Toleration and the Constitution.* New York: Oxford University Press, 1986.

Ritchie, David G. *Natural Rights.* 1894. Reprint. London: George Allen and Unwin, 1952.

Robinson, Lillian S. *Sex, Class, and Culture.* Bloomington: Indiana University Press, 1978.

Ross, Stephen David. *The Nature of Moral Responsibility.* Detroit: Wayne State University Press, 1973.

Rothbard, Murray. *For a New Liberty.* New York: Macmillan, 1973.

Russell-Smith, H. F. *The Theory of Religious Liberty.* Cambridge: Cambridge University Press, 1911.

Sabine, George H. *A History of Political Theory.* 3d ed. New York: Holt, Rinehart and Winston, 1961.

Safilos-Rothschild, Constantina. *Women and Social Policy.* Englewood Cliffs, N.J.: Prentice-Hall, 1974.

Searle, John. *Speech Acts.* Cambridge: Cambridge University Press, 1969.

Seligman, Edwin A., ed. *Encyclopaedia of the Social Sciences.* 15 vols. New York: Macmillan, 1934.

Shambaugh, Bertha M. H. *Amana: The Community of True Inspiration.* Iowa City: State Historical Society of Iowa, 1908.

Shue, Henry. *Basic Rights: Subsistence, Affluence, and U.S. Foreign Policy.* Princeton: Princeton University Press, 1980.

Simpson, George Eaton, and T. Milton Yinger. *Racial and Cultural*

SELECTED BIBLIOGRAPHY

Minorities: An Analysis of Prejudice and Discrimination. New York: Harper and Brothers, 1953.

Singer, Peter. *Democracy and Disobedience.* Oxford: Clarendon Press, 1973.

Skinner, B. F. *Beyond Freedom and Dignity.* New York: Alfred A. Knopf, 1971.

Slawson, John. *Unequal Americans: Practices and Policies of Intergroup Relations.* Westport, Conn.: Greenwood Press, 1971.

Smith, Adam. *The Wealth of Nations.* Edited by Edwin Cannan. New York: Modern Library, 1937.

Smith, T. V. *Beyond Conscience.* New York: McGraw-Hill, 1934.

Soble, Alan, ed. *The Philosophy of Sex: Contemporary Readings.* Totowa, N.J.: Rowman and Littlefield, 1980.

Stephen, James Fitzjames. *Liberty, Equality, Fraternity.* London: Smith, Elder, 1873.

Sullivan, John L., James Piereson, and George E. Marcus, *Political Tolerance and American Democracy.* Chicago: University of Chicago Press, 1982.

Sumner, W. G., and A. G. Keller. *The Science of Society.* 4 vols. New Haven: Yale University Press, 1982.

Thernstrom, Stephen, ed. *Harvard Encyclopedia of American Ethnic Groups.* Cambridge: Harvard University Press, 1980.

Tinder, Glenn. *Tolerance: Toward a New Civility.* Amherst: University of Massachusetts Press, 1976.

Van Loon, Hendrik. *Tolerance.* Boni and Liversight, 1925.

Walzer, Michael. *Just and Unjust Wars.* New York: Basic Books, 1977.

———. *Obligations.* Cambridge: Harvard University Press, 1970.

SELECTED BIBLIOGRAPHY

Wasserstrom, Richard A. *Today's Moral Problems.* 2d ed. New York: Macmillan, 1975.

————, ed. *Morality and the Law.* Belmont, Calif.: Wadsworth, 1971.

Wolff, Robert Paul. *The Poverty of Liberalism.* Boston: Beacon Press, 1968.

Wolff, Robert Paul, Barrington Moore, Jr., and Herbert Marcuse. *A Critique of Pure Tolerance.* Boston: Beacon Press, 1969.

Zielinski, Thaddeus. *The Religion of Ancient Greece.* Translated by George Rapall Noyes. Freeport, N.Y.: Books for Libraries Press, 1971.

Articles

Banerjeb, S. P. "Tolerance and a Secular State: The Indian Perspective." *Indian Philosophical Quarterly* 12 (April–June 1985): 177–90.

Childress, James F. "Appeals to Conscience." *Ethics* 89 (July 1979): 315–35.

Crull, Sue R. "Possible Decline in Tolerance toward Minorities." *Sociology and Social Research* 70 (October 1985): 57–62.

Doppelt, Gerald. "Walzer's Theory of Morality in International Relations." *Philosophy & Public Affairs* 8 (Fall 1978): 3–26.

Ericsson, Lars O. "Charges Against Prostitution: An Attempt at a Philosophical Assessment." *Ethics* 90 (April 1980): 335–66.

Fotion, Nick. "Paternalism." *Ethics* 89 (January 1979): 191–98.

————. "Speech Activity and Language Use." *Philosophia* 8 (October 1979): 615–38.

Gardner, Barry S. "Rawls on Truth and Toleration." *Philosophical Quarterly* 38 (January 1988): 103–11.

187

SELECTED BIBLIOGRAPHY

Goldman, Alan. "Plain Sex." *Philosophy & Public Affairs* 6 (Spring 1977): 267–87.

Grief, Gary F. "Tolerance and Individuality." *Journal of Value Inquiry* 8 (Spring 1974): 30–36.

Halberstam, Joshua. "The Paradox of Tolerance." *Philosophical Forum* 14 (Winter 1982–83): 190–207.

Hare, R. M. "Principles." *Proceedings of the Aristotelian Society*, n.s., 73 (1972–73): 1–18.

Harrison, Geoffrey. "Relativism and Tolerance." *Ethics* 86 (January 1976): 122–35.

Harrison, Jonathan. "Utilitarianism and Toleration." *Philosophy* 62 (October 1987): 421–34.

Hartenberg, S. J. "Extremism and Tolerance in Politics." *Ethics* 77 (July 1967): 297–302.

Hearn, Thomas K., Jr. "On Tolerance." *Southern Journal of Philosophy* (Summer and Fall 1970): 223–32.

Hocutt, Max. "Must Relativists Tolerate Evil?" *Philosophical Forum* 17 (Spring 1986): 188–200.

Ickheiser, Gustav. "On 'Tolerance' and 'Fanaticism': A Dilemma." *Philosophy and Phenomenological Research* 29 (March 1969): 446–50.

Ihara, Craig K. "Moral Skepticism and Tolerance." *Teaching Philosophy* 7 (July 1984): 193–98.

Keenan, James F. "Prophylactics, Toleration, and Cooperation." *International Philosophical Quarterly* 29 (June 1989): 205–20.

Kolenda, Konstantin. "Freedom and Tolerance." *Humanist* 48 (March–April 1988): 38.

Kurtz, Paul. "Ethical Forum: Participation, Bureaucracy, and the Limits of Tolerance." *Humanist* 29 (November–December 1969): 16–20.

SELECTED BIBLIOGRAPHY

Lang, Gerel. "Tolerance and Evil: Teaching the Holocaust." *Teaching Philosophy* 7 (July 1984): 199–204.

McCutcheon, Allan L. "A Latent Class Analysis of Tolerance for Nonconformity in the American Public." *Public Opinion Quarterly* 49 (Winter 1985): 474–88.

Mahler, Halfdan. "People." *Scientific American* 243 (September 1980): 67–77.

Miller, Steven D., and David O. Sears. "Stability and Change in Social Tolerance: A Test of the Persistence Hypothesis." *American Journal of Political Science* 30 (February 1986): 214–36.

Newman, Jay. "The Idea of Religious Tolerance." *American Philosophical Quarterly* 15 (July 1978): 187–95.

Pitts, Edward I. "Spinoza on Freedom of Expression." *Journal of the History of Ideas* 47 (January–March 1986): 21–35.

Richards, David A. J. "Toleration and Free Speech." *Philosophy & Public Affairs* 17 (Fall 1988): 323–36.

Sampson, William A. "Desegregation and Racial Tolerance in Academia." *Journal of Negro Education* 55 (Spring 1986): 171–84.

Searle, John. "A Taxonomy of Illocutionary Acts." In *Expression and Meaning*, pp. 1–29. Cambridge: Cambridge University Press, 1979.

Smith, Wade A. "Cohorts, Education and the Evolution of Tolerance." *Social Science Research* 14 (September 1985): 205–25.

Stafford, J. Martin. "A Rejoinder to Professor Edgley." *Journal of Philosophy of Education* 15 (December 1981): 171–74.

Terborgh-Dupuis, Heleen. "The Netherlands: Tolerance and Teaching." *Hastings Center Report* 14 (December 1984): 23–24.

Waldron, Jeremy. "Theoretical Foundations of Liberalism." *Philosophical Quarterly* 37 (April 1987): 127–50.

SELECTED BIBLIOGRAPHY

Walkling, Philip H. "The Idea of a Multicultural Curriculum." *Journal of Philosophy of Education* 14 (June 1980): 87–95.

Wall, James M. "Beyond Toleration to Equal Rights." *Christian Century* 104 (April 29, 1987): 395–96.

Wilson, Thomas C. "Urbanism and Tolerance: A Test of Some Hypotheses Drawn from Wirth and Stouffer." *American Sociological Review* 50 (February 1985): 117–23.

Index

INDEX

About the Authors

Nick Fotion is Professor of Philosophy, Emory University. He received his B.S. from Northwestern University, his M.A. from State University of Iowa, and his Ph.D. from the University of North Carolina. His publications include *Ethics* (1968), *Moral Situations* (1968), *Military Ethics* (1986, with Gerard Elfstrom), *Military Ethics: Looking Toward the Future* (1991), and an edited volume *Hare and Critics* (1988, with Douglas Seanor).

Gerard Elfstrom is Assistant Professor of Philosophy, Auburn University. He received his B.A. from Cornell College and his M.A. and Ph.D. from Emory University. His publications include *Military Ethics* (1986, with Nick Fotion), *Ethics for a Shrinking World* (1989), and *Moral Issues and Multinational Corporations* (1991).